The Power of
Parent–Child Conversations

The Power of
Parent–Child Conversations

*Growing Your Child's Heart and Mind for
Success in School and Life*

Jeff Zwiers

ROWMAN & LITTLEFIELD
Lanham • Boulder • New York • London

Published by Rowman & Littlefield
An imprint of The Rowman & Littlefield Publishing Group, Inc.
4501 Forbes Boulevard, Suite 200, Lanham, Maryland 20706
www.rowman.com

6 Tinworth Street, London SE11 5AL, United Kingdom

British Library Cataloguing in Publication Information Available

Library of Congress Cataloging-in-Publication Data Available

ISBN 9781475860542 (cloth) | ISBN 9781475860559 (ebook)

Contents

Introduction

This book is *not* about preparing your child to "get ahead" of other children. It is not a race against others to be reading first, to solve fifth-grade math problems in first grade, or to go to a ranked college at age fifteen or eighteen. It is not a competition, and when it becomes one, it often becomes harmful. Nor is this book about the latest "surefire" fad in child raising. It does not intend to reform how you are currently raising your child. It simply offers ideas that you can add to your already heavy "parenting toolbox." The main tools that you will find in this book focus on helping your child to think, to talk with others, to care for others, and to learn more effectively in school.

In the initial stages of my work on this topic, I was reticent to offer parents suggestions on how to talk with their children. I thought it would be too intrusive, given the wide variety of conversations and family dynamics out there. Yet as I talked with parents about this topic and noticed their interest in improving their conversations with children, more and better reasons emerged for putting my findings into a book. Here are four of them.

The first reason is to answer questions that keep surfacing in my work with many different parents and in my own parenting. These include:

- How can I improve my skills for having more productive conversations with my child?
- How do I help my child improve his or her conversation skills?
- How can I make conversations with my child as strong as they can be for building our relationship?
- How can I have conversations that prepare my child for academic success?
- How can I have conversations that prepare my child for life?
- How can I use conversations to grow my child's skills, habits, and traits for being a happy and caring person throughout life?

Hopefully, some of these questions will be answered to varying degrees in the following chapters.

The second reason is to help children succeed in school. I am an educational researcher, teacher, and parent. I spend most of my time immersed in conversations with children and teachers. I observe a wide range of children in school and out, and I spend a lot of time watching how students learn, how their minds develop, how they use language, and how great teachers teach. Much of my mental energy is devoted to children who are "struggling" to do well in school. Many of them "struggle" because they have not had hefty helpings of school-like reading and talking at home.

In my work in schools, I have noticed that children have a wide range of challenges. When they come in with lots of homegrown language, knowledge, social skills, and thinking skills, they are more likely to succeed. What happens at home makes a big difference, and a large chunk of this difference comes from conversations.

Being prepared for school actually means several things. First, children need to have a lot of the language that is used in school. This, however, doesn't mean that they need to speak English at home. Students in non-English-speaking homes actually do much better when parents converse with them in their home language. Second, children have to be ready to do the many tasks that school requires, such as listening to complex ideas, following directions, taking tests, working with others, answering questions, reading, and writing. And third, children need to know how to learn. This means authentic *learning*—not just doing well on tests. Conversations can prepare children in all three of these.

This book emphasizes helping you have *academic conversations* with your child. These are conversations that help your child work with others to co–build up meaningful ideas, concepts, and claims in their minds.

The third reason is to help children have happy and fulfilled lives. Of course, school isn't everything. I also wrote this book because there are many children (and adults) who, for a variety of reasons, are not where they could be socially and relationally. Many children (and adults) lack empathy and the abilities to engage in even simple conversation with others. This stems from a variety of reasons, one of which is time spent using screens (video games, social media, TV, etc.).

Children need to learn how to be good family members, friends, partners, work colleagues, community members, and citizens of the world. And conversations are the lifeblood of relationships. To have healthy relationships, children need to develop good traits and values, and they need to reduce bad traits and values. They need to learn how to interpret and predict the feelings of others while doing the same for themselves.

You can use conversations to help your child's mind gravitate toward the healthier and more positive focuses in life, such as helping others and engaging in certain hobbies. As you can see from the "planets" in the diagram (figure 0.1), there are lots of not-so-healthy topics that can tug our minds in different directions. For some people, certain topics are actually black holes that consume all other things. The widths of the arrows, which vary across people, represent the strength of the pull of the topic. We do not want our children's minds, now or later, to be dragged down by (i.e., dwell on) the harmful or time-wasting topics. We can use conversations as a tool for highlighting the topics that are more fertile for the healthy growth of young minds and hearts.

The fourth reason is to improve the world. Good conversations can change the world for the better. When people understand one another and how others think and feel, the world improves. When people learn to work together to solve big problems, the world improves. When good conversations shape children, they grow into adults who are better thinkers, friends, and family members.

Consider the opposite. When people don't know how to talk with one another, bad things tend to result. The daily news, for example, is full of these bad things. We should want to make the world a better place because

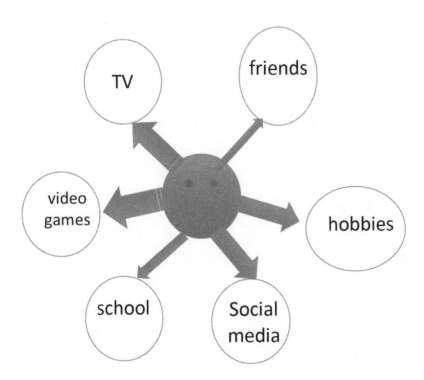

Figure 0.1.   Forces That Tend to Shape and Tug for a Child's Attention

we are here, and we should want our children to want this too. Growing our children's hearts and minds through conversations can help.

Chapter 1 introduces several core ideas related to conversations and how they shape young minds. Chapter 2 describes the various conversation skills that help conversations to thrive. The next four chapters help parents and caregivers have conversations about stories, history, science, and math. These are the four main subjects that students learn in school. The final chapter focuses on using conversations to grow the hearts of children, which means developing their feelings, values, and traits.

All of the chapters provide suggestions and "idea seeds" for expanding and enriching conversations with your child. My hope is that this book will help you identify and improve some aspects of how you converse with your child. Some of you might want to have more conversations each day; others might want to increase the length or quality of your conversations, come up with more interesting topics, better prepare your child for school, or a combination of these.

Chapter One

Conversing to Cultivate Your Child's Mind and Heart

Conversation is cultivation.

Your child's mind is a lush garden of thoughts and feelings that thrive on rich conversations with others. These thoughts and feelings are much like vines and flowers, trees and shrubs, mosses, and weeds. They sprout up, spread out, get tangled up, and blossom in ways that you never expect.

Conversations act like seeds, sunlight, water, and fertilizer for a young mind. During conversations, you often provide new questions and ideas to talk about, which are like seeds that will take root and grow over time. For example, think about your ideas about poetry, friendship, nature, culture, music, art, language, work, school, and so on. These ideas started small and grew a lot from many conversations with others.

And just as sunlight is vital and daily, frequent conversations are necessary to nourish the mind and the heart. Conversations give your child's brain the needed daily language, social connection, and practice with ideas that foster growth. Conversations also allow you to see what your child does and doesn't understand so you can fill in the gaps along the way, somewhat like the giving of water and fertilizer to plants to help them grow. You provide much of what your child's mind and heart need to grow, such as experiences, stories, descriptions, and rich conversations.

And the soil is you. You are solid, fertile ground for your child to build up ideas, try out language, and see how you consistently think about the world. As you converse, your child learns from you how to clarify, support, nego-tiate, and build ideas with another person. You do a variety of things to shape and guide the conversations. Notice how the father does some shaping and "gardening" in the following conversation.

Father: How'd you like the book?

Daniel: It was good.

Father: What was it about?

Daniel: Polar bears.

Father: What about them?

Daniel: How they're running out of ice.

Father: How?

Daniel: The big icebergs that they float on, you know, at the North Pole. They're melting.

Father: Oh, yeah, I have read about the ice up there melting. The bears need the ice to hunt, right?

Daniel: Yeah, and I think to live . . . but I think 'cause it's warmer each year now, it's all melting, but I don't know why.

This was not a very long conversation, but you could see how the father used it to nudge Daniel to think and talk beyond four or five short turns, which is common for a conversation that starts out with "How did you like . . . ?" The father added some knowledge about the bears hunting and prompted Daniel to come up with a question at the end about the causes of the melting ice.

As a parent, you play a large role in the daily growth of your child's mind. And yet, around half of the influence on your child's mind and heart is genetic. You have no control over this half. Sorry. But the other half, more or less, is nurture and experience—which you can influence. Conversations play a large role in this influencing. Just one conversation might not do a whole lot, but many good conversations over time can make a big difference in how your child thinks, feels, and interacts with others.

Physically, "you are what you eat," but in many ways, mentally, you are what you think about, and you often think about what you talk about. Therefore, the more thought-provoking conversations your child has, the more mental growth there will be. This includes growth in language, knowledge, empathy, and social skills.

You make many split-second choices in each conversation. At different points, you say some things instead of other things; you ask a question instead of directly explaining; you listen instead of arguing your point; you focus on the topic instead of jumping to a new one; you empathize instead of criticizing; and so on. Building the skills and habits of saying the best thing—or nothing—at the right times in conversations is one of the main goals of this book.

Keep in mind that this book can only include a limited set of conversation samples from a small cross section of the total population of the world. You and your child may have very different conversation styles and language backgrounds from the samples here, and you don't know the backgrounds of the many parents and children whose conversations you will see. But you can learn a lot (I have) from the snippets of their conversations because they illustrate a variety of conversation skills and topics.

THE NEED FOR BETTER CONVERSATIONS

Life is full of social situations, jobs, tasks, and relationships, all of which depend on talking with others. School, for example, often requires children to work together in conversations to accomplish learning tasks. Outside of school, conversations tend to have clearer and more authentic purposes, such as making a decision, arguing a point, solving a problem, and creating new ideas. And yet, despite the needs, many children grow up struggling to have high-quality conversations with others. Why? Here are few reasons.

Quantity and Quality of Conversations at Home

Research on child development tends to argue that parents need to talk more with their kids. Most parents would agree that they need to increase the quantity of talk with children. Yet experts also emphasize the importance of quality. For example, Hirsh-Pasek and colleagues (2015, 1082) found that quality of interactions more accurately predicted children's later language use than did the quantity of words heard from caregivers. The researchers found three important features of quality during parent interactions with young children:

- joint engagement with the use of words and gestures
- routines and rituals that provided predictable patterns for making meaning
- how well a parent and child stayed on topic throughout an interaction

These features can help you begin to form an idea of what quality conversation is in your family—and how to increase it by using the ideas in this book.

Quantity and Quality of Conversations in School

Classroom lessons vary a lot, but there are many commonly used activities such as reading, writing, listening, answering questions, and participating in discussions. These academic activities and skills depend a lot on a child's oral language and thinking skills—which are highly influenced by conversations. Some of the juiciest classroom conversations, for example, depend on thinking skills such as hypothesizing, interpreting, summarizing, comparing, evaluating, making decisions, arguing, identifying causes and effects, and/or taking different perspectives. When these skills are cultivated at home, there is more learning at school.

Much of my research consists of observing conversations between students in elementary and middle school classrooms. I have observed many different conversations between students in all grade levels. As I observe their conversations, I analyze how well the students are communicating ideas, asking questions, listening to and building up ideas, caring about what a partner says, and using conversation skills in appropriate ways. I have seen that most students—even the students who score well on tests—need to improve their face-to-face conversation skills. And I have seen many students improve their reading and writing over time as a result of having more and better conversations.

Quantity and Quality of "*Non*-Face-to-Face Conversations" (e.g., Social Media)

Face-to-face conversations are being influenced by large chunks of time using social (which some call *antisocial*) media and online communication tools. You have likely seen and participated in the many "*non*-face-to-face conversations" that happen in blogs, chats, e-mail, text messages, Facebook, and Twitter, for example.

Social media can serve a range of needs, and it even sparks some good conversations at times. Social media has fostered many exchanges of information between people because of the ease of posting comments electronically. However, many virtual "conversations" are shallow, short, unfocused, awkward, negative, time-consuming, biased, and even manipulative.

Children often use devices to send messages to each other. Texting, for example, is popular even for younger children. You can find plenty of arguments both for and against texting (and blogging, chatting, tweeting, etc.). Some say that such communication motivates children to write and read. Others say it hurts their spelling, grammar, and abilities to communicate longer messages. Even sending pictures (e.g., Instagram) is another form of communication, but more research is needed to understand how conversational it is.

Excessive screen use can deprive your child of many important things that only happen in face-to-face interactions with real people. These important things include developing abilities to use facial expressions and body language, collaborating to create and explore ideas, responding in real time to an idea offered by a person, thinking on their feet, clarifying ideas for others, and supporting ideas with credible evidence, to name a few.

BENEFITS OF HAVING GOOD CONVERSATIONS WITH YOUR CHILD

Conversations Help Your Child Succeed in Life

"Success" comes in many flavors. The type of success emphasized in this book is a mixture of happiness, fulfillment, and service to others. These elements of success don't depend on making a lot of money, scoring high on reading tests, getting into top universities, or getting prestigious jobs. I will consider my children, for example, to be successful if they feel that they are happy, doing what they think they were meant to do in life, approaching and reaching their potentials in different areas, loving and serving others to the fullest, having strong relationships, having plenty of choices, and making good decisions. Conversations play a large role in fostering these aspects of success.

Conversation Builds Your Child's Knowledge

The more knowledge your child has, the more likely he or she will do well in school and in life. Knowledge includes facts, definitions, and information about how things work in various subject areas such as history, science, math, literature, and so on. If your child knows that caterpillars turn into butterflies or that northern states fought southern states in the Civil War or that one-eighth is smaller than one-third, he or she is better prepared to learn related knowledge and skills in school. In fact, many of the most successful students learned a lot of their knowledge outside of school.

Your child's knowledge tends to come from books, movies, television shows, experiences, and conversations. You can't control all of the knowledge that goes into your child's mind, but you can influence some of it. You can talk with your child about what he or she is learning and thinking about. You can help your child realize that the mind thrives when it is used to talk about topics in depth over time.

You can use conversations to emphasize the kinds of knowledge that help them in school and to prune the types of knowledge that just clog up the brain. For example, many video games, TV shows, and social media sites are full of negative and mindless content. What goes into the mind often stays in the mind—especially, for some reason, the worst stuff.

Conversations can foster your child's curiosity, which can be a lifelong force for learning new knowledge. The more things that your child talks about, the more exposure he or she has to new ideas that might interest him or her. Conversations are opportunities for (a) your child to express interests and confusion and (b) you to clarify and explain concepts. For example, your child might observe a crescent moon. You might ask what she wonders about, and she asks, "Why does it change shape every night?" This starts a conversation about orbits, light, and shadows that can ignite further interest in space and science.

Conversation shapes what your child thinks about. Conversations generate energy, questions, and mental images that keep the mind thinking about whatever the conversation was about. So if your child talks a lot about what's wrong with friends, school, and the world or talks for hours about video games and television shows, these topics will linger in his or her mind.

What's on your child's mind most of the time? Much of who your child is now and is becoming is what he or she thinks about during the day. Therefore, have conversations that get your child to think about things that matter. Even though keeping your child from bad TV shows, websites, and video games definitely helps, it is also vital to talk about a wide range of meaningful topics that help your child grow into a great person.

For example, several meaningful topics that parents talk about are solving problems in the world, helping friends, expressing ideas through art and music, appreciating the beauty and wonder of nature, hypothesizing causes and effects in nature, interpreting themes in stories, creating stories, and so on. The following chapters present many additional topics, some of which are more school-based and some of which are more life-based.

Conversations Foster Your Child's Thinking Skills

Not only do conversations shape *what* your child thinks about but also *how* your child thinks. The most important skill is building up ideas, which are usually either claims (e.g., school uniforms are necessary) or concepts (e.g., lots of animals use camouflage to survive). Other academic skills that should be used to build up ideas (i.e., not taught separately) include analyzing, evaluating, applying, empathizing, comparing, inferring causes and effects, hypothesizing, summarizing, synthesizing, supporting ideas, and arguing. Chapter 2 offers more detailed descriptions of these skills.

Conversations Nourish Your Child's Heart

Knowledge and thinking only get you so far, as any interaction with a social-ly awkward person or an evil mastermind will tell you. The heart is the center of your child's emotions, values, and traits, which are shaped and nurtured by conversations with you. Unfortunately, there are a lot of other influences, especially in movies, TV shows, video games, and social media, that can wreak havoc on a child's heart.

Violence, sarcasm, greed, racism, lies, and narcissism abound, and they are trying to shape and tear down your child's emotions and abilities to empathize. You can use conversations to cultivate important feelings that reside in the heart, such as gratitude, patience, joy, forgiveness, and a will-ingness to share, to name a few. For example, your child might talk about a kid who bullies others at school. You can have conversations about how to feel about the situation.

You want your child to develop traits that help him or her to be a good person. Such traits include perseverance, curiosity, creativity, empathy, kind-ness, flexibility, appreciation, confidence, humility, honesty, and patience. Feel free to add others to this list. For example, I want my children to have the habit of seeing the good in people. I also want them to think about how they can help others, rather than just focus on themselves.

Conversations can also help children more clearly see the value in impor-tant things such as justice, family, friends, honesty, spending time with oth-ers, communicating, sharing, art, nature, learning, honesty, and commitment.

Conversations Develop Your Child's Social Skills and Relationships

Conversations offer you a chance to model conversation skills, and they offer your child a chance to practice them. The more conversations he or she has with you (and with others) the more chances there are to be pushed to com-municate ideas, support them, and compare them. Conversations can help your child to:

- think more about the needs and perspectives of others
- learn from others
- more clearly describe his or her own ideas to others
- solve problems
- empathize with others
- accomplish tasks in collaboration with others

You can and should build up your child's skills at shaping conversations with others. Rather than letting others (including you) always do the shaping and guiding of a conversation, your child needs to build up his or her own abilities to do so. This means being able to initiate a conversation, keep it going, prompt for evidence in support of ideas, stay focused on its purpose, and prompt partners to stay on topic.

Conversations Develop Language

Conversations require your child to listen and talk many times. Every other turn, your child hears language coming out of your mouth. You adjust what you say as your child shows signs of understanding or confusion. You might use a long sentence or big word and have to break it down or use easier words. All the while your child is expanding his or her language by listening to you.

On the flip side, every other turn requires your child to think and put an idea into words. This provides lots of real practice with language. With a real person (you) listening to every word said by your child, he or she is forced to communicate clearly. If you don't understand something, you let your child know. He or she might then rephrase or repeat the idea. Or you might offer new words, grammar, or ways to be clearer.

A good conversation pushes your child to both comprehend and use new language in real time with a real other person. Each turn, your child must overcome mini-challenges to understand and be understood because he or she is, in a sense, half of the "total workforce" that is engaged in constructing a new idea or making a new decision.

You can also use conversations to encourage your child to try out new words and expressions. Notice in the following conversation how the father models and encourages his daughter to use new language.

Father: What is that?

Maya: Grifbeet.

Father: What is grifbeet?

Maya: Food for you.

Father: Wow, it looks delicious. Can you say that?

Maya: Delish.

Father: What are the ingredients?

Maya: What?

Father: Ingredients are the things it is made of. What ingredients are in it?

Maya: Ingredients are half a triangle and chocolate chips.

Father: I can't wait! It sounds delicious!

Conversations Strengthen Your Relationship with Your Child

Conversations allow you to share who you are with your child and vice versa. As your child gets to know you, you get to know your child. Conversations are great ways to show and grow love between you and your child. Conversations allow a two-way sharing of passions, concerns, interests, questions, ideas, and trust that will help your child know and feel connected to you.

Conversations Help Children Feel Valued and Listened To

In lives saturated with duties and distractions, children can feel that people (including parents) don't listen to them or value their ideas. Conversations are chances to show your child that you value his or her ideas, no matter how confusing or strange they are. As you talk face-to-face with your child, making eye contact and showing interest and excitement, you help to reinforce your child's imagination, self-confidence, and creativity.

Conversations "Fill in the Things" That Teachers Don't Have Time For

It takes a lot of conversation time to get good at conversations. In school, a lot of class time needs to be used doing things other than conversation (e.g., reading, writing, etc.), and because of this, (a) we can't rely on school to teach our children how to converse with others, and (b) we need to help our children work on their "academic conversation" skills at home as much as we can. Of course, children also do better in school when they learn a lot of literacy (reading and writing), content (math, history, science, etc.), and language at home—all of which are better developed through conversation. Conveniently, most of this book is focused on helping you do this.

CHALLENGES TO OVERCOME

Defining Conversations

Unfortunately, *conversation* suffers from a wide range of definitions. Many online and even in-person "conversations," for example, jump quickly from topic to topic and do not build up ideas. They look like decent conversations on the surface, but they often lack direction, depth, details, support, and clarity. Many "conversations" are also dominated by one person who tries to push his or her ideas on others (e.g., a parent pushing an idea onto a child).

Hopefully, after reading this book and practicing some of its ideas in conversations with your child, you will have a better idea of what good conversations are between you and your child. Likely, your evolving definition will include some of the skills and behaviors mentioned in this and the following chapters.

Conversations Vary Wildly

One of the big challenges of writing a book on this topic is that conversations vary very wildly. They vary from family to family, country to country, and hour to hour. You can talk about a topic at 5 p.m. with your child and then at 6 p.m. talk about the same topic with him or her and have a completely different conversation. It is therefore impossible to memorize a few bullet points and think you have mastered conversations. We must instead build our skills and habits much like master artists and professional athletes do, over time.

Also, many of the sample conversations in this book come from a limited number of families and situations. Conversations between children and parents from thousands of cultural, geographical, and socioeconomic backgrounds could not be included in this short book, for obvious reasons. Thus, the sample conversations in the following chapters are only meant to show certain ways in which some parents converse with their children.

You will have a wide range of conversations with your child. Your child is complex and unique, and so are you. Your conversations have been, are, and will be different from those in this book and those of the people next door to you. But my hope is that, by looking at these samples and the extra information around them, you will walk away from this book a little more excited and equipped to have more and better conversations with your child.

Genes

Just ask any parent who has raised two or more children and they will tell you that genes make a difference. Some parents are shocked at the differences in spite of the same upbringing, culture, schooling, and so on. Many siblings differ drastically in a myriad of ways, including how they talk with others. Therefore, conversations should add to, amplify, and foster the growth and potential of each child.

And yet, like a gardener, you can use conversations to fertilize certain areas and to prune others. You might use conversations, for example, to foster your child's curiosity, knowledge of biology, ability to argue respectfully, and skills of clarifying ideas. You might also use your conversations to reduce selfishness, arrogance, gossip, and negative attitudes.

Your Child's Interactions with Others

You will not always be around when your child is interacting with friends, classmates, teachers, and relatives. From others your child will learn good and bad ideas, good and bad language, and good and bad habits of communicating and thinking about the world. Your job is to (a) have enough good conversations with your child to counteract the "bad" stuff that they might pick up from others; (b) try to expose your child to people who will be good for your child; and (c) model how to have good conversations with others.

Seeing the Results

You won't likely notice any changes in your child after one conversation or even after a month of good conversations, but over longer periods of time you will see their effects. Some effects, as I mentioned before, are due to genes and some come from typical maturation, but a large portion is shaped by conversations with you. This long-term shaping places a large burden on us parents. We usually can't just "have a conversation" that fixes things right away. We need to have many conversations over time. We need to listen and be as consistent, caring, and creative as we can be.

Here are some other features you might include in your evolving list of what should happen in good conversations with your child:

* positive and encouraging messages
* valuing one another's ideas
* asking for elaboration and clarification
* encouraging the use of clear language
* supporting ideas and opinions
* encouraging a variety of perspectives and opinions
* building up of ideas that weren't in their minds before talking
* empathy
* nonverbal engagement and active listening

SUMMARY

Growing young minds through conversation is hard and messy work that continues for many years. There are no perfect conversations, and we will never know precisely how they affect our children's hearts and minds. There are many variables other than conversations that shape your child's development, but we know that conversations play a large role, and we can usually improve them. One of our jobs as parents is to cultivate our children's minds and hearts in ways that help them cope with challenges, make good choices, succeed in relationships, and value the "right things" as they live their lives. Our conversations with them are vital for this job.

BIBLIOGRAPHY

Hirsh-Pasek, Kathy, Lauren Adamson, Roger Bakeman, Margaret Tresch Owen, Roberta Michnick Golinkoff, Amy Pace, Paula Yust, and Katharine Suma. "The Contribution of Early Communication to Low-Income Children's Language Success." *Psychological Science* 26 (2015): 1071–1083.

Chapter Two

Developing Conversation Habits, Skills, and Mindsets

Conversations need solid foundations.

If you haven't done much reflecting on how to improve the quality of conversations with your child, this chapter can help. It offers foundational "suggestions" for improving the most important conversational habits, skills, and mindsets.

MAKE SURE EACH CONVERSATION HAS AT LEAST ONE PURPOSE

Many parents see conversations as a way to change a child or to "download" information into the child. How many of you have heard a parent say, "You and I need to have a conversation about . . . " while the parent was actually thinking, "You need to change, and I'm going tell you how"? And many of us have a tendency to think in this way too. Yet true conversations focus on building up ideas together, not just the child listening or answering a parent's questions with answers that the parent wants to hear.

Both you and your child should know, at least roughly, the purpose(s) of a conversation. The obvious reason for this is that, because you are building up ideas together, you can be productive and co–build up an idea. Table 2.1 shows different types of purposes for conversations that you might have with your child.

Not all conversations will start off with clear purposes, but it helps to try to come up with at least one rough purpose for each conversation at some point early on. It can help to keep in mind the types of purposes you see in

Table 2.1.   Types of Purposes for Conversations

Conversation Purpose	Sample Conversation
To grow your relationship with him or her	Parent: Could you relate to any character in the movie? Child: To Zach because he was afraid of the water but then realized it was safe. Parent: I also related to Zach but because he was shy with friends at school, like I was when I was young. Child: What did you do?
To solve problems together	Child: Why do people have war? Parent: Great question. I ask that all the time. One reason is because they want the same thing, like land. Child: Can't they share it? I share my toys with Sophie. Parent: They could, but they want it for themselves.
For both of you to practice conversation skills	Parent: What do you mean when you said you don't like bees? Usually it helps to explain why you don't like something. Child: They sting people. Alex poked a bees' nest and got stung yesterday. Parent: They usually don't sting unless they are bothered. What if a person poked a big stick into our house? Child: What do you mean?
To build knowledge and concepts	Parent: You want to build a racing car, huh? Do you know what a car race is? Child: You and me drive the car. Parent: We could, but usually it's one driver who tries to drive faster than all the other cars to get to the finish line first. They usually drive around the course many times. There are also running races and even horse races.
To model and practice thinking skills	Child: Some video games are good. Like Minecraft. Parent: How is it good? Child: You need to solve problems and make things, like tools. Parent: Is it better than reading? Child: I have to read a lot to play the game. I read to build things. And I still read books, too.

Conversation Purpose	Sample Conversation
For both of you to build character traits, attitudes, and values	Child: I hate math. Parent: Why? Child: 'Cause I'm no good at it. Parent: You can get better at everything; some things take time and patience. Child: And it's boring. Parent: Maybe we can work together to help you get better at it, and then it might not seem so boring. And even if it is a little boring, a lot of things in life are necessary. My job is boring sometimes, but I still do it. Child: Like doing the dishes and folding the clothes? Parent: Exactly.

table 2.1. Having a purpose builds up your habits of reflecting on the quality of conversations during and after you have them.

KEEP SHARPENING *YOUR* CONVERSATION SKILLS

Most people don't sit around and think about what makes conversations good or bad or how to improve them. The best conversers, young and old, tend to use six core skills to engage in great conversations. The skills are described here, and you will also see them a lot in later chapters.

Skill 1: Listening

Listening is a foundation for the other conversation skills. Listening to your child shows that you value what he or she says, which is very helpful as your child tries out new ideas and ways of communicating them in conversations. It's effectively working *with* your child to accomplish the conversation's purpose(s).

Good listening includes nodding, making appropriate eye contact, and short responses such as *Wow! Huh?* and *Really?* It also includes making sense of what you hear and thinking about how it fits into the conversation's direction and idea building (which is Skill 2). For example, your child might say, "I don't think it was right to feed those birds." You could agree and add to it and so on, but you instead ask more questions to help her clarify and support her idea (Skills 4 and 5). Along the way, you nod your head and say "Interesting! Wow!" and so on to show how much you value what she says.

There are several things you can do in conversations to help to model and build your child's and your listening skills. These include:

- paraphrasing what your child said and asking, "Was that what you meant?"
- asking your child to paraphrase or summarize what you just said
- reminding your child to show listening with eye contact, head nodding, etc.
- using a "talking stick" or other token that you pass back and forth (the person holding the token talks while the other listens)
- encouraging your child to ask clarifying questions during the conversation (What do you mean by . . . ? Why . . . ?)

Skill 2: Building Up at Least One Meaningful Idea

Every conversation should build up at least one meaningful idea. This means that you and your child take turns and exchange information in order to build up an idea that wasn't there or wasn't as built up before.

An idea could be a concept, claim, conclusion, understanding, reason, and so forth. An idea is meaningful if: (1) when your child says it in a sentence, you want to know more, and/or (2) it needs a paragraph or more (e.g., a chapter, a book) to describe it well. For example, if your child says, "I think the story teaches us to keep trying," you likely want to know more. You might ask clarify (Skill 4) questions such as "What does ___ mean?" or support (Skill 5) questions such as "Why? What are examples from the story? What are examples from your life?"

You and your child will tend to use Skills 4 and 5, clarifying and supporting, to do this building.

Meaty ideas come in many shapes and sizes. A few examples include:

- The moon doesn't really change its shape.
- We should lower the voting age.
- A fraction is part of one whole.
- Seeds need water and sun.
- Grandmothers are wise.
- We should share.
- People need to work to pay for food.
- Animals survive by hiding or escaping.
- Airplanes and birds need wings to fly.
- Clouds are like steam from a teapot.

Notice that these ideas are not just simple facts or preferences such as "The banana is yellow"; "I like cookies"; "The dress looks nice on you"; "I don't want to go to bed"; "The sun is hot." Some of the bulleted ideas are claims and some are concepts, but they all are buildable, meaning that two people who talk about them can add their own clarifications and support.

You can start with statements like those in the list and converse with your child to shape them into a more buildable idea: "I wonder why fruits are different colors." "Why do cookies rise up and expand when they bake?" "Why do clothes look good or not on people?" "Why is sleep so important for our bodies?" "How does the sun's heat help all people and animals and plants on Earth?" The answers to these questions will tend to be longer and more buildable. And many answers will be helpful for building up content knowledge for school.

Often your conversation ideas will come up as a result of experiences, reading, watching, and so forth. Your child might ask, "Why do birds fly?" This question offers a chance to talk about animal adaptations and even human inventions such as the airplane. As you read the previous sentence, you probably thought, "Wait, there are a lot more interesting directions a conversation could go." True, a question like that could spark a wide range of conversations.

Skill 3: Posing Buildable Ideas

Encourage your child to ask lots of questions and pose different opinions and ideas. Then try them out in conversations. Work to build them up and see what happens. *You* should also model the posing of different questions and buildable ideas. You and your child can find ideas all around: in books, in magazines, online, on TV, in museums, in movies, in parks, and so on. If your child is in school, there are many potential ideas in the homework and texts that your child brings home.

Skill 4: Clarifying Ideas

Clarifying ideas means doing things to make a topic or idea less abstract, more usable, and more understandable. Clarifying often involves elaborating, explaining, paraphrasing, and asking questions. If you ask your child how her day was, and she says, "Bad," you will likely ask her to clarify by asking something like "Why?" or "What do you mean by *bad*?" If your child over-assumes that you know what they are talking about, they will often say as little as possible.

You clarify an idea because you and another person usually have differing ideas of what something is or means. Children especially often assume that you know exactly what they are saying, even when they say just one word. And you, as a parent, have had a lifetime of experience building up meanings for words that your child hasn't had yet. Clarifying also often relies on sub-skills such as narrating, defining, using gestures, and even drawing.

Then again, you might have a very talkative child who under-assumes that you know what he or she is talking about. Talkative children can say too much, which therefore requires some paraphrasing on your part. And of course, *you* might say too much, and therefore, you need to (a) paraphrase yourself in order to clarify what you are saying or (b) encourage your child to ask clarifying questions or paraphrase what you said (but don't do it in a harsh "now you better paraphrase what I said so I know you got it" way). Here is a sample conversation with lots of clarifying.

1 Mother: What did you learn in school today?

2 Raquel: About ants.

3 Mother: What about them?

4 Raquel: They live benext to each other.

5 Mother: What does that mean?

6 Raquel: They live in holes all together. They make little hills with, with the dirt they dig up.

7 Mother: They call that a colony, when insects or any large group of animals live together. They have different jobs.

8 Raquel: Yeah. I think there's the queen and the workers.

9 Mother: How do workers know what to do?

10 Raquel: I don't know. I'll ask the teacher. But I'm not sure how anyone would know. Ants don't talk.

11 Mother: But they do communicate, I think.

12 Raquel: Maybe like with their antennas?

Notice the prompting for clarifying and the clarifying in lines 3 through 12. This conversation, like many, could have ended in line 5, with a parent saying, "Interesting. Now let's have a snack," but this mother pushed for clarification and a much more powerful conversation resulted.

Skill 5: Supporting Ideas

Supporting an idea means using examples, evidence, or reasoning to strengthen it. Supporting ideas is a very important skill to have for school and life. For example, you can't just say your opinion and expect others to agree (unless you are a politician or a professional athlete in a TV ad, of course).

We all need to support what we say. With conversations, you can apprentice your child into knowing what is good evidence and what is not. For example, "Because I saw it on TV" doesn't hold much water when arguing a point in school or the workplace. In fact, I have seen that one of the biggest "gaps" in school is not test scores. It is the gap between the students who do and don't (a) see the need to support ideas; (b) critically evaluate the strengths and weaknesses of evidence; and (c) work hard to support ideas as much as possible. Here is a sample conversation in which the father is helping his son improve his support skills.

Father: Can you tell me about a dinosaur?

Chris: A spinosaurus. It was big and catched fish.

Father: Interesting. How do you know that it caught fish?

Chris: Like their bones?

Father: What about their mouths?

Chris: They had mouths like alligator mouths.

Father: So like long mouths, right? And alligators catch fish. What about where they live? I mean lived.

Chris: Maybe they found fish in their mouths?

Father: Maybe, but I think more likely the scientists found bones near what was water back when they lived.

Chris: Maybe like they got stuck in the mud and died by a lake.

If your child says, "We should watch a show about pandas," you can ask, "Why?" in order to get him to support the idea with a reason or an example.

Skill 6: Evaluating Evidence and Reasons

When there is an argument or decision to be made, you converse to build up the competing ideas, and then you choose one. It is helpful to emphasize *collaborative arguing*, which means (a) working together (i.e., not trying to *win* the whole time) to build up all sides of an argument or decision and then (b) weighing the evidence and reasons on each side to choose the "heavier" one. You both *evaluate* the weight of the evidence and compare the overall weights of each idea to choose the stronger or "heavier" one.

Often, your child's values and your values will differ when you are evaluating evidence—and there will be many other feelings mixed in too. Common values that come out of my mouth, for better or worse, are "Because I want to keep you safe"; "It's too expensive"; "We don't have enough time"; "You need to sleep so you don't get sick"; "Because in life we need to learn how to be patient"; "I value your ideas and what you have to say"; "I love your creativity"; "It's important to clean up our messes"; and so on.

A helpful visual for seeing and doing this is an argument balance scale, shown in figure 2.1. If there are two competing ideas (Should we get a puppy or not?), you put each idea on each side of the scale. Then you put reasons and evidence in the boxes on each side. You and your child then discuss the value ("heaviness" or strength) of the evidence for each idea and pick the side that, overall, is heaviest or strongest.

Here is a sample conversation between a mother and her daughter.

Mother: What are you thinking about?

Deja: I want a puppy.

Mother: Why?

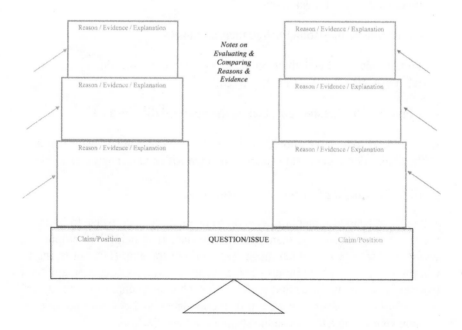

Figure 2.1. Argument Balance Scale Organizer

Deja: 'Cause I want one.

Mother: Yes, but what are some good reasons to get a puppy?

Deja: It'll be fun.

Mother: OK. What else? Why would it be better to have a puppy here than to not have one?

Deja: I can learn to take care of it.

Mother: OK, any other reasons?

Deja: No.

Mother: I can think of one. It would be good for a puppy to have a wonderful person like you to care for it.

Deja: Yeah.

Mother: Now, what are reasons for *not* getting a puppy?

Deja: They're messy.

Mother: Yes. Especially until they are potty trained.

Deja: And it costs money to feed them.

Mother: And pay for visits to the veterinarian.

Deja: That's it.

Mother: Well, also, it will be tougher to be away, even for a weekend.

Deja: Yeah.

Mother: So which side weighs more? Which reasons are bigger overall?

Deja: Getting a puppy.

Mother: Why?

Deja: I'll learn to be responsible and we'll give a puppy a great home.

Mother: Is that heavier than the costs in time and money?

Deja: Yeah.

Notice how the mother helps guide Deja in building up both sides of the argument and then evaluating and comparing them near the end. As you can see, there are a lot of personal values involved in evaluating, especially in more emotional topics and decisions such as this one. As kids get older, you can introduce the use of criteria to help them compare evidence and reasons. So when you tell your child to "make a good choice," this process can help your child know how to choose and explain why.

Pro-Con

This is a short and fun activity that you can do with your child to get him or her to talk about both sides of an issue or argument. You choose an issue or topic with two sides (pros and cons) and make sure your child has some of the topic's pros and cons in mind or at least on paper to look at. Then say the topic and "pro" to prompt your child to come up with a positive. Your child should not just say a word or short sentence in each turn (e.g., "Dogs play with you") but also add sentences to the turn that elaborate, clarify, and support with examples (e.g., "For example, dogs like to play fetch and wrestle"). Then after the first pro turn, say "con." Optionally, have your child start the next turns with "However," "On the other hand," or "Then again." Optionally have your child make an "on the other hand" hand motion in which your child touches the opposite elbow, palm down, and lifts it in an arc the other way, ending with the palm up. After the multi-sentence con turn, go back to pro and repeat until the ideas are done. Feel free to give your child "idea seeds" to elaborate on and prompt for clarification and examples when needed. Optionally, at the end you can tell your child, "I think you leaned on the side of . . . because . . ." For fun, switch roles to have your child be the director and you say the pros and cons.

STRIVE TO HAVE MORE AND BETTER CONVERSATIONS OVER TIME

We should always be trying to increase the quality of our conversations. A high-quality conversation means that it helps your child learn something, practice communicating, get to know you better, feel more confident and valued, learn to converse with others, and/or be more prepared for school and life. In a low-quality conversation, your child might feel less valued, learn bad or wrong things, get confused, or see negative ways of relating to others. Most conversations, though, are somewhere in the middle of the spectrum between high and low. A good goal to have is to nudge all conversations toward the high-quality side over time.

It's hard to "measure" the improvement of your conversations. But there are a few things you can try to notice: number, length, and quality. *Number* means the quantity of conversations with your child over time. Were there more or fewer this month? *Length* means that the average conversation occupies more time or has more turns in it. It can also mean that your child is using longer turns. You can try to compare these from month to month. For example, last month, with my oldest child, I had fewer conversations than the previous month, but the ones we did have were longer. Her turns seemed to be longer, and some were even extra long.

Improving *quality* means that each month the conversations are a bit deeper, more interesting, more impactful, and so on. It might mean that your child is using more thinking skills such as interpretation, empathy, cause and effect, application, comparison, or logical argumentation. It can also mean that you and/or your child are using more conversation skills such as posing buildable ideas, clarifying, supporting, and evaluating the strength of ideas, as well as using nonverbal skills such as eye contact, gestures, and posture. It might also mean that your child is doing more of the prompting for clarifying and supporting ideas.

Another dimension of conversation quality to improve is the use of language. Is your child using (saying and understanding) more precise words and more complete sentences? Is your child using (saying and understanding) more complex sentences and connecting them with terms such as *for example, in order to, even though, on the other hand, because,* and *despite*? If not, you can model their use over time.

Finally, you can roughly measure quality by thinking about the topics being discussed. Are this month's topics more engaging, more applicable to life, more complex, more academic, and so forth?

HAVE ENDURING TOPICS AND THEMES TO TALK ABOUT

Conversations don't always begin and end in one day. They can last weeks, months, and even years. These enduring idea conversations can play a large role in the growth of your child's mind because they keep deepening and clarifying a topic over time. The repetition and revisiting of the topic helps its key points and language to stick in your child's mind better than just one conversation could do.

Whenever you hear yourself say, "Now, we've talked about this before" or "We need to have another chat about . . . ," you might want to put the topic on your enduring idea list. Here are a few topics that you can consider putting on your list:

- being humble, confident, forgiving, obedient, diligent

- delaying gratification
- practicing to improve
- caring about others
- doing your best
- considering how others think and feel and empathizing
- being a team player
- being a good friend
- not believing everything on the Internet
- using scientific methods (making cause-effect hypotheses, isolating variables, etc.) to verify ideas

For example, over the years, I want to keep talking with my children about the following big idea topics:

- being honest, unselfish, and patient
- being happy with who they are and what they have
- doing their best
- thinking about how causes and effects happen in nature
- looking for life lessons in stories, poems, songs, and visual arts
- not judging people by how they look

You can use daily situations as springboards to talk about these ideas. For example, my child and I might be walking through a park and we see a big tree with acorns underneath it. I say, "Look at all those acorns! I wonder why there are so many," which starts a conversation about seeds, what happens to most of them, and how they grow.

Here is a sample conversation in which the mother is continuing to emphasize the enduring idea of being a team player.

Mother: How did the game go?

Bella: We lost, and it was Gaby's fault. She missed the ball.

Mother: Remember, Bella, what we have discussed about being a team player.

Bella: Yeah.

Mother: It doesn't seem like it, though.

Bella: We tried but . . .

Mother: Your team lost. It wasn't Gaby. It's a team sport. You have made mistakes, too. Remember when you picked the ball up?

Bella: Yeah.

Mother: So what do we need to remember about teamwork?

Bella: It's about learning how to work hard and help each other.

Mother: And making friends. And Gaby already feels bad. Do you want her to think she is losing her friends because she made one mistake in a game?

Bella: No.

Notice (a) how the mother reminded Bella of what it means to be part of a team and (b) how she had Bella take the perspective of her friend to feel what she might be feeling.

HAVE LOFTY GOALS FOR YOUR CHILD'S MIND AND HEART

You likely already have rough goals for your child's thinking and feeling. Sure, you want to be flexible and not hem in your child's growth too much, but it helps to keep thinking and feeling goals in mind when conversing with your child. When listening to a story, for example, you might want your child to be thinking about how the main character feels and if other people in the world feel this way. You can also have "don't" goals. Some parents don't want their children to be critical of the main character's intelligence; others don't want their children to give up easily when facing challenges.

It might help to write your "do" and "don't" goals down and keep track of them. And you will get some additional ideas in the following chapters. These goals can change over time and may never be fully reached, but they will help to guide you in what you say and do to nudge your child toward the types of thinking that help him or her in life.

You can start by thinking about what you want your child's mind to do in different situations. For example, when playing a game, singing a song, walking through a forest, reading a book, or watching a movie, consider what you would like your child to be thinking. This will shape your conversations. Of course, more often than not, your child will be thinking of something very different from what you intended, and you must go with the flow. But at least the goals you have in mind can influence what you say in conversations.

Table 2.2 lists a few of the goals that you might want your child to think and feel as they grow into young adults. The list will likely change over time, but it can give you some direction. Make your own list—and then, for fun, see how well *your thoughts and feelings* match up to it.

Of course, not every conversation has to have goals in mind. Just talking with your child about a wide range of topics is important. But I suggest storing heart and mind goals in your head for when you see conversational opportunities to develop them. For example, the goal of being more patient (for my child and for me) comes up aplenty every day in our household.

GROW *YOUR* MIND AND HEART

Many of your thoughts and feelings have been shaped throughout the years by conversations with others. Likewise, your thoughts and feelings shape the conversations that you have with your child. Thoughts about politics, history, science, soap operas, fishing, money, spy novels, cars, movies, hobbies, or food, for example, tend to influence your conversations.

In too many cases, what happens at work occupies your thoughts and shapes your conversations because of the hours that your mind has spent thinking about it. You tend to talk about what you think about. And you tend to think about what you do, watch, and read. And yet, for most children, talking about your work or the news isn't very interesting.

Is what goes on in your mind a good model for your child? Do your thoughts linger on things that you would like your child to think about too? Are you thinking about making money, worried about the future, worried about the furniture, angry at coworkers, complaining about the stresses of the day, concerned about appearances, and so on? The things that you think about tend to surface in conversations.

But how you think and what you think about can change. Just spend some time at the end of the day reflecting on what you thought about and talked about most of the day. And then set some goals for the next day. Possible thinking goals include seeing the beauty of nature, being more creative and doing more art, having more conversations about your child's ideas, being much more patient, and showing more excitement about being with them.

Table 2.2.   Sample List of Mind and Heart Goals

Mind	*Heart*
• Think of creative ways to solve problems • Collaborate well with others • Ask questions about why things happen • Use evidence and reasons to support arguments	• Think about the well-being of others • Share things and ideas • Be patient • Be forgiving • Be nice

SUMMARY

This chapter provided a set of foundational skills, habits, and mindsets for improving conversations over time. These are things to keep working on throughout life. You need to keep figuring out the purposes of conversations with your child, along with ways to improve *your* conversation skills over time. Finally, it helps to come up with effective goals for your child's mind and heart and be looking out for ways to best grow your own heart and mind.

Chapter Three

Conversations about Stories

When wrapped in conversation, a great story becomes a cherished gift for the soul.

Stories are powerful shapers of young minds. For thousands of years, they have changed how children think, feel, and grow. After reading or listening to a story, a child might become more inspired, more confident, more informed, or more intrigued by how others in the world think, live, and feel. Of course, a lot of helpful shaping can and does happen without talking to others, but the benefits can be even more powerful through conversations.

After describing several important benefits of conversing with your child about stories, this chapter offers ways to (a) use conversations to build up key habits for understanding stories and (b) use several practical strategies for deepening conversations about stories.

BENEFITS OF CONVERSING ABOUT STORIES

Better Mental Movies

Conversations can help children better visualize what is happening in a story, making, in a sense, a movie of it in their minds. Conversations about what they are picturing in their heads can help them verbalize their thoughts, add detail to their mental movies, and resolve any confusions they might have. And starting with picture books, children begin to see how characters and events are woven together to create engaging stories that hold readers' attention. They can use the pictures in the book to help get them started in making a movie of the story inside their minds.

Your child puts scenes together and visualizes what happens to the characters over the course of the story. Conversations can help children strengthen these visualization skills. By talking about what is happening, your child can learn to put together scenes that he or she has never seen and "play movies" in the mind based on the story. For example, in the following conversation about *The Paper Bag Princess* (Munsch, 2018), notice how the father helps Paulina see beyond the picture on the page.

Father: So what is going on in the story?

Paulina: I don't know. She is sad. She lost her castle and Roland.

Father: And all she could wear was a paper bag! Wow!

Paulina: And she was brave.

Father: How so? What brave things did she do?

Paulina: She went to the dragon's cave. And she talked to him and got him to get tired out.

Father: Describe it to me. I will close the book. Imagine I didn't read it or look at the pictures.

Paulina: Well, she knocked on the big door and the dragon stuck his big nose out. Then she had him burn a lot of forests, maybe to use up his fire. And then she got him to fly and get really tired. He flew fast with his wings, around the world.

Father: Why did she have him do all that?

Paulina: I don't know. Wait. Let me see. Oh, maybe to save Roland. That was smart of her, I think.

Father: And then Roland made fun of her for wearing a bag. Can you believe that?

Paulina: She should have left him in the cave.

More and Better Knowledge

Stories are doorways to vast warehouses of wisdom and truth. Talking about stories can teach children about many things that they don't learn from school, life experiences, or even online videos. Stories also offer a wide range of new ideas, scenes, characters, problems, emotions, events, time periods, and places. Stories help children to expand how they look at the world, what's important, what success means. It helps them expand their imaginations—and their options—for who they want to be and how they want to live.

Many stories are too challenging for solo reading, which is actually helpful, because conversations can address the challenges and clarify questions. For example, you might be reading a story with a theme of being honest. As you read the story to your child, you stop to talk about parts where the main character isn't honest and why it causes problems. But then you also bring up the question, "What if the problems that came up didn't happen? Would it then be OK to be dishonest?" This question might prompt a discussion on doing the right thing, such as telling the truth, in order to be a good person.

Look at the following conversation to see how much potential there is for learning science concepts from a story.

Mother: Do you think there are aliens?

Edgar: Maybe. I seen lots of aliens on stories and TV.

Mother: Yes, it's fun to read stories about aliens and other planets. They're made up to make the stories more interesting. Like you said, maybe there are aliens, or life on other planets, but we haven't found it or seen it yet.

Edgar: Why not?

Mother: Good question. Because we haven't been able to go to all the planets. There are billions of them, and they are really far away. Each star is like our sun and might have planets orbiting around them.

Edgar: What's a billion?

Mother: It's a thousand millions; it's a lot. Like if you count the sand in the sandbox. So with so many planets, maybe on one of them, at least, there's like some plant life or animals.

Edgar: And they maybe have people with three legs and four arms. And pink plants instead of green.

Mother: That would be interesting, right? I would like to see alien life, but I don't want to take the time to travel there.

Edgar: How long does it take?

Mother: Years and years. Some planets are like a thousand light-years away. That means it takes a thousand years to get there, if you go the speed of light, which is really fast.

Edgar: A thousand years? I don't want to do that.

Notice how this conversation offered a chance for Edgar to learn about large numbers, probability, planets, stars, space travel, and the fact that all aliens in books and on video are fictional—according to the government, that is.

Increased Emotional Growth and Empathy

Children often become emotionally involved in good stories. They tend to care about the story's characters and even empathize with them. Children can learn how a wide range of others respond to different situations and challenges and life. And conversations can further deepen children's emotional awareness and empathy in response to reading literature.

Stories can help readers step into the minds and hearts of other human beings, many of whom are thousands of miles away, speak different languages, have very different backgrounds, or even lived long ago. Stories can also help students overcome feelings of isolation because they can see that others have experienced similar feelings, challenges, and triumphs.

Here is a short conversation that stemmed from the reading of *Holes* (Sachar, 2000). Notice the focus on feelings.

Father: How did you feel when Stanley was sent to the detention camp?

Isaiah: It wasn't fair.

Father: How do you think he felt?

Isaiah: Sad. I think like no hope, too. Like he couldn't do much. And he was cursed.

Father: Cursed?

Isaiah: Yeah. His great-grandfather did something.

Father: So if you feel cursed, maybe you don't try as hard?

Isaiah: Yeah. But I wondered if he would get back at Zero after he found out he was the one who stole the shoes and maybe back at the warden for being so mean.

Father: How did it work out?

Isaiah: It all worked out in the end.

Father: How did you feel about the ending?

Isaiah: I felt happy because Stanley was nice and got to help Zero and they got away from the camp. And the curse was broken.

Stronger Thinking Skills and Reading Strategies

Stories also help children to build important thinking skills such as figuring out causes and effects, interpreting character motivations or life lessons in a story, and taking different perspectives. Good readers think about why things happen in a story and why characters do and say things. This skill, of course, helps them in the "real stories" of real life. This means that they can more easily and quickly figure out the who, what, why, how, and "How important is this?" elements of daily living—a vital skill that even adults haven't fully developed.

As children read or listen to stories, they see problems arise and wonder how they will be resolved. They ask questions, make predictions, make inferences, and want to read on. They become curious about what will happen.

Stories also help children interpret how to be better people and solve big problems in life. And stories get children to think about other time periods, problems, perspectives, and how other people feel and live life. This helps children to build empathy and the ability to take different perspectives, which are major skills for developing your child's heart (see chapter 7). These things can get much stronger with conversation. For example, in conversation, you can help your child look at what characters are doing and saying in order to think about how we can be better human beings.

Notice how conversations like the following one can help develop students' thinking skills and reading strategies (*The Rainbow Fish*, Pfister, 1999).

Mother: What was the Rainbow Fish like in the beginning?

Emma: He didn't want to share his . . .

Mother: Scales?

Emma: Yeah.

Mother: Why?

Emma: I don't know. He liked them.

Mother: And I think he wanted to be more beautiful than all the other fish. But what happened?

Emma: His friends didn't play with him 'cause he didn't share.

Mother: Then he finally shared, right? And how did he feel?

Emma: Good. And his friends played with him.

Mother: So what can we learn from the story.

Emma: It's good to share?

Mother: I think that, too.

More Developed Language

Stories provide lots of rich language that is rarely used in daily social interactions. Just look at a children's book and you will find many words and sentence that you don't use or hear when you talk to others during the day. With repeated exposures, your child's mind soaks up new language for later use in reading, writing, listening, and talking. In fact, many of the language differences between students come from differences in exposure to and immersion in stories that they have read and listened to. Notice the vocabulary and grammar used in the following conversation about the novel *Because of Winn-Dixie* (DiCamillo, 2000).

Father: So do you think the author was trying to teach something to us with this story? In other words, what's a theme or moral to teach us how to be better people?

Daniela: I don't know. Opal was lonely and didn't have friends. And then the people she met in the new town were a little weird.

Father: Hmmm. So they weren't the friends she expected to have, right?

Daniela: Yeah.

Father: What about the dog, Winn-Dixie? I think he was important, especially because of the title of the book, right?

Daniela: Winn-Dixie was lonely, kinda like her. But he was friendly to everyone, like the preacher.

Father: Wow. He loved people *even* when they didn't seem to like others. How is that a lesson for us?

Daniela: Maybe we should love people, even if they're a little weird.

Father: Yes, and maybe a nicer word for them is *eccentric* or *different*.

USING CONVERSATIONS TO BUILD HABITS FOR UNDERSTANDING STORIES

One of the biggest challenges in school is understanding difficult stories. While some children have sound-letter (phonics) and grammar-based challenges, many need to bulk up *comprehension habits*. Good readers, listeners, and watchers have comprehension habits that kick in automatically as they read, listen to, or watch a story. You can have conversations with your child that help to build these habits. In fact, the earlier a child builds these habits, the better prepared he or she is to read in school.

Habit 1: Identifying Main Characters

Your child should build the habit of identifying main and minor characters. Most stories have one or more main characters that do, think, and say things that make the story a story. Your child needs to be able to quickly figure out who the main characters are as well as what they are like on the outside and, often even more important, what they are like on the inside.

Characters will often change in some way on the inside (their motivations, personalities, values, and feelings) during a story. Identifying these changes is a key skill required of students in school. Think about the many stories that you have read and the kinds of things that main characters have learned or how they have changed throughout the story.

How to Develop This Habit through Conversation

- Have your child think about the title, look at the cover, and skim through the pictures to guess the main character(s). Then read to find out.
- When watching movies or TV programs, ask who the main characters are and talk about why they are important.
- Talk about how the main character changes during a story.
- Ask, "How do you think he/she/it needs to change?"

Here is a sample conversation that focuses on identifying main characters.

Father: Who are the main characters in this story?

Elena: The toys.

Father: Why?

Elena: 'Cause they talk and they need to go somewhere.

Father: What about the trains?

Elena: They don't look like people.

Father: But they talk and think, right?

Elena: I guess so. The blue train kept saying, "I think I can."

Father: And he made it over the mountain, right? Would you say he's the main character? And remember the title of the story. That's important, too.

Elena: Yeah.

Habit 2: Identifying the Main Conflict, Problem, or Challenge and Its Solution

Most stories have a central problem that main characters struggle to solve, often overcoming little challenges or "obstacles" along the way. Most stories also have a climax and solution to the problem, followed by final explanations. Just think of most movies, which often have one or more main characters overcoming obstacles to reach a goal.

You can help your child build the habit of seeing what authors want readers to see as the main problem or challenge in a story, which is not always obvious. There can often be a main external problem (e.g., defeating the bad guy) and a main internal problem (e.g., learning to love, forgive, or be humble). External events and internal changes often influence one another.

How to Develop This Habit through Conversation

- Ask, "What is the biggest problem that needs to be solved in this story?" If your child mentions a minor one, ask for other possibilities or share your idea as a model.
- Ask, "Do you think that the main character has to change in his/her mind or heart?"
- Ask, "Why do you think this problem is bigger than other problems in the story?"

- Ask, "What do you think the story would be like without this problem?"

Here is a sample conversation about the story *The Day It Snowed Tortillas* (Hayes, 2003) that helps the child focus on the biggest overall problem in the story, not just some of the minor hurdles.

Mother: What is the biggest (main) problem that needs to be solved in this story?

Sam: The thieves wanted to steal their money?

Mother: That was a problem, but it was just at the end. What was the woman's problem during the whole story?

Sam: Hmmm. Her husband wasn't smart, and he talked too much.

Mother: So what did she not want him to talk about?

Sam: Their money.

Mother: So what did she do? Did she keep him from talking about the money?

Sam: No. He talked about it. But she made him sound, like, crazy because she put tortillas out and he thought it snowed tortillas.

Mother: And the thieves didn't believe him about the money, right? So she solved the main problem by being clever, right?

Habit 3: Determining Importance and Summarizing

Readers need to quickly recognize what is important and unimportant in a story. So what makes something important? Most often, it is information that is needed for the plot, character development, or themes (if any). If you took the information out of the story, it would change it in a major way. Children can over-focus on exciting and juicy parts of story, yet these might be less important details and events. Conversations can help guide your child to focus more attention on the important information.

Summarizing means putting the important information into usable and memorable chunks. Since the brain can't hold every single piece of new information at any given moment, good readers summarize the ideas and events on different scales: paragraphs, pages, and even whole chapters.

How to Develop This Habit through Conversation

- You can stop during reading and have your child summarize the most important parts up until that point. Ask, "Is that important? Why?" If your child chooses an unimportant detail, discuss why it is not very important to the story and model how you choose more important parts.
- Have your child stop reading after one, two, or several pages and summarize what has happened since the last summary or from the beginning.
- Ask, "What just happened?" or "What should we remember from these pages?"
- Have your child retell stories that he or she read, listened to, or watched. (This is also a common practice in school.) During retelling, you can ask, "How was that part important to the story?"

Here is a sample conversation that helps build the child's abilities to choose important details and summarize.

Mother: I can tell that you liked that story. Tell me the important things that happened.

Tania: Marty was a Martian, and he came to visit Earth.

Mother: Interesting. So a true story?

Tania: No.

Mother: So why was that important?

Tania: He wanted to learn about Earth, and he met a boy, Edgar, who showed him.

Mother: So why was that important?

Tania: 'Cause later he asked Edgar to go with him to Mars. He always wanted to go to Mars. He was bored on Earth.

Mother: Oh. That sounds important. So Edgar was bored; then what happened?

Tania: Edgar showed Marty lots of flowers and trees and mountains. He never saw them on Mars. He thought they were beautiful.

Mother: So did he go?

Tania: No.

Mother: That sounds important. It's a big decision, right?

Tania: Yeah.

Mother: What did Edgar learn that would be good for us to learn, too?

Tania: I think to see how beautiful things are, like trees and flowers and things.

A related skill is keeping track of time in a story. Some of the more complex stories jump around between past, present, and future, and if you don't keep track of where you are in the time line, it gets confusing. And authors often like to use foreshadowing and flashbacks, which can make comprehension even more difficult if children are not used to them. Even adults (like me) sometimes have trouble recognizing these features.

Habit 4: Predicting

Predicting means thinking about what will happen in the story. This is often what we do when we start reading a novel, watching a TV show, or listening to a spouse tell a story about work that day. To predict, a reader uses existing clues, such as titles, pictures, and any previously read texts. The reader mixes knowledge about similar situations with the new clues in the story to predict something. Predictions can include events, changes in characters, and even themes. Predicting is powerful because it sets up a "win-win" mental situation: if the prediction is wrong, there is mental energy devoted to comparing the wrong prediction with the right outcome; if the prediction is right, there is mental energy devoted to having the prediction confirmed. This mental energy fosters learning.

How to Develop This Habit through Conversation

- You can first look at the title and cover art and ask your child what he thinks the story will be about. You can ask what will happen, how the characters might change, what they might learn, and even what the life lesson of the story might be.
- You can ask your child to think about previous stories and what happened in them. This gets the prediction muscles warmed up.
- You can also thumb through the book (do a "book walk") and have your child do some further predicting.
- When reading, after each page or two, have your child predict some more. You can also model your predictions at times.

Here is a sample conversation that helps build the child's abilities to make helpful predictions while reading a story. Before reading the story *Are You My Mother?* (Eastman, 1960), Manjit and his father were looking at the picture on the cover of a dog and a bird. Notice how the father pushes for more complete predictions and reasons for them.

Father: What might this story be about?

Manjit: A dog and bird.

Father: OK. So the story might be about the bird or the dog or both. Keep both in your mind and we'll see what happens on the next page to get an idea of what might happen. (reads next page)

Manjit: The bird going to find mother!

Father: Why do you think that?

Manjit: He ask and ask all animals. They tell him.

Habit 5: Making Inferences

An inference is really just a prediction in reverse. It means being a detective. You use current clues to guess what happened before. Because the author never tells readers everything, we need to infer and fill in the holes with our own thinking. In order to keep readers' minds engaged, the author might purposely leave things out for readers to fill in and infer. For example, an author might not include the details about the main character's upbringing on a farm, even though readers need to assume some of these details to form an idea of the character. In other cases, the author might assume that readers will make inferences needed for understanding the story. Readers who have read a lot generally make such inferences, but some readers miss out because they have life and reading experiences that are very different from those of the author.

How to Develop This Habit through Conversation

- Ask a lot of "Why do you think . . . ?" questions while reading. "Why do you think the character said that?" "Why do you think she did that?" "Why do you think he feels sad?"
- You can model your own inferences when needed.
- Remind your child of what happened to him or her as it relates to making an inference. "Remember when you put your blanket on the ice to melt it? What happened?"

Just before this conversation, the mother had told a story based on what happened to a friend of hers (David) in school many years before. Notice how she uses her story to bring up a similar situation happening in Keisha's school.

Mother: Why do you think people didn't like my friend David?

Keisha: I don't know. 'Cause maybe . . . 'cause he liked bugs?

Mother: Maybe. But why wouldn't people like him because of that?

Keisha: Maybe they didn't like bugs. They crawl on you and sting you. I don't like goin' around lookin' for bugs, either.

Mother: I think that, too. And maybe also they didn't like him because he didn't play the same games at recess with other kids. Do you know anyone like that?

Keisha: There's a girl at school; she just sits and reads at recess.

Mother: Why do you think she does that?

Keisha: She likes to read, maybe, but also she doesn't make friends.

Mother: You could go and ask her what she is reading, maybe become her friend. I think she would like to have a friend like you.

Keisha: Maybe we could talk about books.

Habit 6: Asking Questions

Your child should ask a variety of questions while reading stories. Questions make your child want to keep reading in order to find the answers. Questions are a bit like rubber bands that, when stretched, give energy to your child's mind. Even though you can encourage and welcome all types of questions, it helps to nudge your child into asking questions that help him or her understand the plot, its themes, and its characters.

How to Build This Skill through Conversation

- Ask your child, "What do you wonder? What do you want to know? What is confusing?"
- Model the types of questions that help your child understand characters, plot, and themes in the story (e.g., What's the big problem in this story?

How does the character change? What am I supposed to learn from this story? Why did the character do that?).

• Show your excitement when you hear good questions from your child.

Here is a sample conversation focused on asking good questions.

Father: So what questions do you have?

Max: Nothing.

Father: The boy is good at growing flowers and can't get these seeds to grow. Do you have a question that starts with "why"?

Max: Why doesn't it grow?

Father: Good question! I was wondering that, too. I also wonder why other kids have big flowers and he doesn't have anything.

Max: Why doesn't he just put new seeds in?

Father: Why don't you think?

Max: 'Cause it's cheating?

Habit 7: Empathizing and Seeing Others' Perspectives

You do not want your child to be someone who has little understanding of how others think, feel, and view the world. This can lead to social awkwardness and isolation. You want your child to care for others, to know what other humans expect, need, and feel. This helps your child connect with them and meet their needs. Talking about stories can help to grow this important part of your child's heart. (See chapter 7 for more on the heart.)

Conversations can help your child build empathy and perspective skills that use three main clues. First, there is the situation: "Given this situation (e.g., winning a big game, a raging fire approaching, strangers arrive on the shore), how do you think the character feels?" Second, your child can use character actions and expressions: "She slumped her shoulders and buried her hands in her face. How was she feeling?" "He dropped everything and ran to find his dog. What was he thinking?" And third, your child can consider what a character says: "She said her tears were a mix of sadness and happiness. Why?" Because many children (and adults) tend to focus on the actions and events in a story, conversing about feelings and perspectives can help to grow this necessary reading habit.

How to Develop This Habit through Conversation

- Ask your child, "How do you think he/she/it feels right now? Why?"
- Model the valuing of others' feelings and perspectives (e.g., "I sure hope she makes friends in that new town").
- Get excited when your child focuses on the thoughts and feelings of others (e.g., "Nice job thinking about how the frog felt about being lost!").
- Extend the conversation by adding slightly different ideas (e.g., "I agree with you that she is sad, but I also think she is mad. Which feeling do you think is stronger in her?").

Here is a sample conversation that develops this habit.

Mother: How do the baby owls feel?

Emily: I don't know.

Mother: What do they say?

Emily: "I miss my mommy."

Mother: So how does the little owl feel?

Emily: Sad. He wants mommy to come back.

Mother: And I think the others are worried that she might not come back. They went out on the branches to wait for her. How would you feel if you were the baby owls?

Emily: Sad and maybe scared.

Mother: But then when she came back, how did they feel?

Emily: Happy, like they are.

Habit 8: Interpreting Themes, Symbols, and Metaphors

One of the most exciting aspects of most stories (and poems, some TV shows, some movies, and most works of art) is their deeper meanings. These are meanings that teach us how to appreciate life and be better people. But most of the meaningful ideas in stories (and life) are not directly stated for readers. Rarely do authors directly tell readers the main lessons or morals of their stories; rather, they let readers figure them out.

Yet many children linger for too long at basic and concrete levels of understanding. In stories, for example, they tend to just think about the plot.

Here is where conversations can help. In conversations, you can share and explain deeper meanings of stories and poems. You can develop your child's interpretation habits so that whenever he or she reads or listens to a story, part of his or her brain clicks into "deeper meanings mode." You can build your child's habit of looking for authors' messages or lessons in every story, even meanings that the author didn't intend.

When readers interpret, they take in observable clues and use their background knowledge to create a meaning that they think is intended but not directly given. Like in the story of the three little pigs, a reader will think of how people might be lazy and take shortcuts, as the first two pigs did, and then think how people take or should take extra time and effort to do something well.

Another more focused type of interpretation is being able to decipher and use figurative language such as analogies, metaphors, similes, symbols, and multiple-meaning words. It is often called *figurative thinking*. Metaphors are ways to make interesting comparisons between two unlike things, usually to emphasize a certain feature of one of the things (e.g., all the world's a stage, love is an ocean, his temper was a volcano). The use of metaphor can open up entire worlds of thought to your child. Not only can your child better understand poetry and literature but content area concepts as well. And many complex concepts in science and social studies can be better comprehended and remembered through metaphor.

Interpreting is a "gatekeeper" thinking skill in school. This means that children must develop this skill in order to succeed in most academic and job settings. Because we live in a world that values information and ideas, your child must be prepared to understand increasingly complex messages, images, and lingo. This necessitates a certain mental flexibility and openness to seeing expressions, connecting to background knowledge, understanding the context, and making meaningful leaps of interpretation.

A few common life lessons, themes, and morals include:

- Treat others how you want to be treated.
- Friendship is more important than money.
- Make the world a better place.
- Talk with people to solve problems.
- Don't judge people by how they look.
- Work hard to reach goals and don't give up.
- Do your best in all you do.

How to Develop This Habit through Conversation

- Model the types of questions that help your child understand themes in the story (e.g., What am I supposed to learn from this story? What is this story trying to teach us? What do you think we should do to be like [or not be like] _____?).

- Share ways in which you would like to change based on life lesson ideas that you read and discuss: "This story reminds me that I need to be nicer to everyone, even people I don't know, like at the store or in the park."
- Get excited when you hear life lesson ideas that your child brings up.
- Ask questions such as "What is this story trying to teach us? What does it mean? How might this help us be better people? What do you think it might symbolize? What did this part mean?"

Here is a conversation that builds theme interpretation skills. It is between a mother and her six-year-old daughter after reading the story *The Empty Pot* (Demi, 1996).

Mother: What did you learn from the story?

Ann: Cooked seeds don't grow.

Mother: True, but what did you learn about life? How to be better?

Ann: Not make fun of others, like when they laughed at him when he couldn't grow a flower. They are mean.

Mother: Yes, it's important not to make fun of others. True. But I was thinking about the end, when he brings the empty pot to the emperor. Did the other kids do what the emperor said to do with their seeds?

Ann: No.

Mother: What did they do?

Ann: They put different seeds in. And then, umm, they put, they brought their own flowers back.

Mother: But they weren't telling the truth, were they?

Ann: They lied.

Mother: So another thing we learned from the story? The emperor was really sad with all those children because they weren't honest. But the boy was honest.

Ann: He was honest and got to be king! So if I'm honest, I get to be a queen?

Mother: No.

These are just some of the vital habits that children need to develop in order to understand and learn from stories. Notice the ways in which conversations can help to (a) model skills and habits for your child; (b) prompt your child to use the skills and describe them to you; and (c) inspire children to think more deeply about stories starting at a young age.

STRATEGIES FOR CONVERSING ABOUT STORIES

Here is a set of strategies that you can use to enhance conversations with your child and to foster the eight habits in the previous section. These strategies are, for the most part, specific to talking about literature and other language arts–focused topics. And if you look at these and think that they look like tasks that children might do in school, you are right. It's one of the purposes of this book, in fact, to equip you with more school-like strategies and tools. They might seem a little too schoolish at first, but try them out and see how your conversations go.

Tell a Story, Ask Questions, and Ask for Questions

You can start by telling a story about what happened today or in the past, or make one up. At times, stop and ask questions. Wait for a response. If your child doesn't respond, you can help by saying, "I bet you would . . . " or "Were you thinking . . . ?" This is particularly effective for younger children who do not use a lot of language yet. Here is a sample conversation between a mother and her two-year-old.

Mother: What did we do today?

Camila: Store.

Mother: Yes, we went to the store. We saw our friend Laura there. She said you had gotten really big. Then we bought some meat and vegetables and fruit. Remember?

Camila: Nana!

Mother: You like bananas and strawberries. Look, here is a strawberry and here is a banana. But you don't like oranges. Maybe someday you will like them. They are very good for you. Then what did we do?

Camila: Car.

Mother: Then we got in the car and drove home. You fell asleep like you always do. I wish you fell asleep that easily when I put you down in your comfortable bed each night. Will you go right to sleep tonight?

Notice the large amounts of language that the child is hearing. Conversations help children to focus on ideas and take in lots of language related to a topic. It offers a chance for you to build up the concept of what a story is and its components, clarify and refine deeper meanings, and reinforce words and grammar.

Use a Plot Diagram

A common visual used in schools is a plot diagram (figure 3.1), also called a story map. It can help you and your child visualize the plot in most stories. The mountain represents the main problem. The little bumps on the way up are obstacles or challenges that need to be overcome on the way to the top when the main problem is solved. Most movies do this. A big problem usually comes up and the main character(s) must overcome trials to eventually solve it, often in a clever way that we didn't expect (even in some action movies). At the end, there is usually some answering of any remaining questions that readers might have.

Here is a conversation that builds plot skills. It is between a father and his five-year-old daughter who are talking about a *Frog and Toad Are Friends* (Lobell, 2003) episode called "The Story." Notice how the father uses a plot diagram to support the conversation.

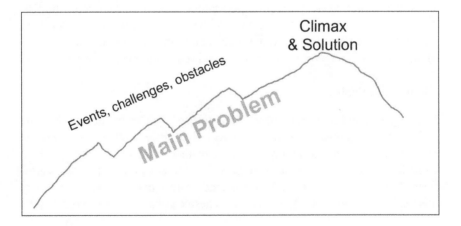

Figure 3.1.   Plot Diagram for the Structure of Many Stories

Father: Remember the story mountain that we drew last week? Let's see if it works for this story. We can draw it real quick. . . . Now, what do we think about finding first?

Elsie: The big problem.

Father: So what do you think is the big problem?

Elsie: I don't know.

Father: What was a problem that they needed to solve?

Elsie: Frog was sick and wanted a story.

Father: But Toad couldn't think of one, right? He tried a bunch of things that we can put on the diagram, right? Like?

Elsie: He stood on his head.

Father: I'll put that here. And?

Elsie: And he walked a lot and poured water on him.

Father: He even banged his head against the wall. These all go on the side here because they aren't the final solution. Does he ever think of a story?

Elsie: No, Frog does. And he tells the story that Toad just did.

Father: Great! We can put that on the top.

Now look at several of the prompts that the father used and notice how he prompted Elsie to think about the parts of the diagram, rather than just asking questions. This helped to reinforce the image of the diagram in her mind and of the rising action that it represents, which is common in most stories.

Theme List Poster

One way to build interpretation skills is to use a poster of themes that you and your child create. It can be a decorative poster and you can put up pictures or phrases that relate to important themes in life, many of which come from stories. This poster then becomes a reference for future conversations. For example, you might have read stories over the past year with themes like the ones on the list below. These can be written in your child's words.

- Noble goals and causes are worth extreme sacrifice and hard work.
- Don't judge people based on appearances.
- Be generous.
- Be honest.
- Be nice to strangers.
- True friendship and love involve deep commitment.
- True beauty is on the inside.
- Diverse ways of thinking and living should be respected.
- Certain symbols in the story represent the main character.
- Being yourself takes courage.
- Differences are needed to make life interesting.
- It's important to have the freedom to become who you want to become.
- Don't be afraid of change.
- Memories are a large part of who we are.
- Don't give in to peer pressure.
- Many people in the world struggle to survive.
- Many stories are based on earlier stories, myths, legends, and so on.
- There is more to life than making money and being comfortable.
- Cleverness can be more effective than brute force.
- Life is short and every day is precious.
- We must preserve the environment.
- Envy and jealousy are destructive.
- People can change for the better.
- There are many types of heroes.
- Standing up for what is right is often difficult and even dangerous.
- Helping others is itself a reward.
- Teamwork is often necessary to do big things.
- All languages and cultures are valuable.
- Respect nature's power and beauty.
- There is hope even when things seem hopeless.
- Peace is possible.
- Set goals and work hard to reach them.
- Older people are often very wise.

Converse to Create Stories

Rather than always just talking about stories that other people have written, try talking about a story created by your child. The process of talking about possible settings, characters, plots, themes, and endings can be fruitful and fun. Here are some suggestions that will help.

1. Ask your child to think of life lessons, themes, or traits that make people better human beings. You can refer to the list of themes earlier

in this chapter. What do good people and heroes do? What are they like on the inside? Can they have flaws? A few starter ideas could be: share, be committed to others, work hard, be honest, keep trying, and so on.

2. Come up with ideas for characters and plots that might be able to show the theme. For example, if the child chooses "Don't lie" as a theme, he might come up with a rabbit that keeps lying and eventually gets caught. Or he might think up a plot in which a boy lies about places he has visited and eventually meets people from those places who ask him questions he can't answer.

3. Decide on the plot and add details to make it interesting. Add events or challenges to overcome along the way. Perhaps add some repetition (e.g., a character meets several animals and asks the same question each time). Converse with your child as you write down the story. Ask why he or she would add certain parts; ask for details, figurative language, different ways to organize sentences, and so forth.

4. Add art to the pages, if possible. Have your child draw, paint, or use images from the Internet or magazines. Talk about the best use of the page and what image to best match the text.

5. If you have your child write a book for a younger sibling, teach your child to read the story extra expressively. Your child can even act like a teacher and stop and ask listeners to react, predict, infer, empathize, compare, and so on. Have your child practice reading with you.

Here is a conversation that somewhat follows these steps.

Mother: What makes someone a good person?

Zaj: Help others.

Mother: So a good person helps others. Like how?

Zaj: He shares toys.

Mother: I like that idea. Maybe we can write a story about sharing. Should we have the characters be people or animals?

Zaj: Animals.

Mother: Which ones?

Zaj: Monkeys? Elephants?

Mother: Let's think about what they can share. Monkeys can share . . .

Zaj: Bananas!

Mother: Yes, and they could also share their trees where they live. Elephants could share . . .

Zaj: Peanuts!

Mother: And they could share the land where they live and water. Remember the show where all animals went to the small watering hole? Did they fight?

Zaj: No, they shared.

Mother: So what about a story? Like what could be a problem?

Zaj: Maybe the elephant doesn't share water.

Mother: And the other animals get thirsty and don't want to be friends with the elephants?

Zaj: And the elephants get sad 'cause they don't have friends.

Personify and Animate: What's Its Story?

You can also pick out daily things and make stories about them. You can have a conversation that creates a little story about the thing. The story might be leading up to what you are seeing right now or it might be from now on or both. You can ask questions that help frame the story (asking for details, motivations, emotions, main conflict, challenges, solutions, etc.).

For example, you and your child might be on a walk and you see a butterfly. Instead of just saying, "How pretty," you can co-create a little story. You can talk about the butterfly's past (its caterpillar days, cocoon time, and the emotions of flight) and/or about the future (where it is going, where it sleeps, how it keeps its colors, etc.). Here is a sample conversation between a mother and her six-year-old.

Mother: Look at that rock. What's its story?

Lisette: It's just a rock.

Mother: But it wasn't always this shape, right? It's smooth and almost round now.

Lisette: It's like rocks at rivers. They're round.

Mother: So what might be a story about it? And let's start it even before the river. Maybe up on a mountain? I'll start. Once upon a time there was a rough rock. She lived on a mountain. Then what?

Lisette: She fell, maybe.

Mother: But why?

Lisette: Wind? Like a big storm.

Mother: Then one day a storm came along and a gust of wind knocked the rock—should we gave her a name?

Lisette: Rachel?

Mother: How 'bout Rachel the rough rock? What happened to Rachel the rough rock?

Lisette: A wind knocked Rachel the rough rock down the mountain.

Mother: And then?

Lisette: It went into the river.

Mother: What did the river do to make her smooth?

Lisette: I don't know. Like she rolled a lot, maybe.

Mother: And other rocks rolled on her. For how long?

Lisette: For lots of years?

Mother: Probably even thousands of years or millions. Then she became Rachel the *rounded* rock, right?

Notice how this conversation not only built up Lisette's sense of story but also helped to build up some of her knowledge of science.

Converse about Wordless Books

Wordless books tell stories with pictures. Often, the stories that you or your child end up seeing will differ a lot—which can actually help your conversation. There are several conversational options. One is to have your child narrate the book as you turn the pages and, at times, have short conversations about what you are seeing and thinking as the reader. As your child narrates the story, you can ask clarifying questions. Or when your child asks a question, you can answer it or say, "Good question. Maybe we'll see the answer later in the story."

You can also have a conversation after the story, as you would about any other story. You can talk about why the author didn't use any words, used certain pictures, and any important ideas or themes that emerged. And you can also talk about any ideas that your child might have for his or her own wordless book.

Here's a sample conversation about the wordless story *Flotsam* (Wiesner, 2006).

1 Father: So why do you think the author didn't use words in this story?

2 Maricela: I think maybe to let us make up the story.

3 Father: Did that work for you?

4 Maricela: Yeah. I liked it. I liked being able to look at the pictures and think up what was happening. Especially when he looked real close at the photograph and saw . . . he saw like pictures of kids in pictures. Each picture had smaller and smaller pictures of kids holding up pictures. I think it was all the kids who found that camera.

5 Father: Weird. But then he threw the camera back in. Why?

6 Maricela: I think for other kids to find. So they could see all the cool things in under the sea.

7 Father: Ooh, and I wonder what new things might show up on the camera.

8 Maricela: Maybe like giant squids dancing on a dance floor?

9 Father: I like that. Or maybe a bunch of crabs playing baseball?

Notice how much thinking and language that Maricela used in this short conversation, especially in line 4. The father also prompted her to think about the advantages of not having words, and he even nudged her to imagine her own interesting scenes inspired by images in the book.

Converse about TV Shows and Movies

First of all, research tends to oppose the watching of TV and movies by children before they are two years old or so (American Academy of Pediatrics, 1999). Infants and very young children are not ready to watch two-dimensional images when they are still learning about a three-dimensional world. Also, most programs have too many words and images for young children to understand, so they get overstimulated or confused or lose interest. Some might even have nightmares from the images they see on TV.

Even if you do limit screen time, your child will likely watch movies or TV shows at some point. First of all, control for content and quality. Most TV is just plain bad. Choose shows and movies that are appropriate, positive, and educational. Ideally, have them watch programs without commercials.

Second, build up your child's abilities to wisely choose what they watch. Talk about the lasting impact of violence and other bad things in most programs. Develop in your child the skill of choosing programs that teach life lessons, communication skills, good character traits, and other positive things. In conversations, help your child to see and avoid the negative content. Remind your child that bad scenes tend to stick in your mind for a long time. And some kids can even start thinking that violence is OK. Do some research and sampling of programs to see what you think is appropriate.

Third, watch alongside your child and think about how to grow his or her mind and heart through conversations about the show. Think about what you will talk about after the show. During the program, you can build up many of the story comprehension habits described in this chapter. You can focus on a key theme, concept, or character. You can encourage your child to come up with questions and build a conversation from there. Ask your child questions similar to those that support reading comprehension.

A downside of TV shows and movies is that, unlike reading, it is harder to stop them in the middle to discuss. If you can, pause the show at times to discuss what is happening, what might happen, and what it means. You can pause shows at key moments to ask plot questions and ask for your child's predictions.

Here is a sample conversation between two parents and their five-year-old son. They had just watched an episode of a show called *Dinosaur Train*. Notice how the parents use the show and conversation to foster Kyle's thinking and knowledge.

Kyle: Why was a shell in the desert?

Father: It was a fossil.

Kyle: What's that?

Mother: That's part of an animal or plant that died a long time ago and it turned into rock.

Kyle: But it was a seashell, so why in the desert?

Father: Why do you think?

Kyle: I don't know. They talked about it was ocean before. But maybe it dried up?

Mother: Remember the *Magic School Bus* episode when they moved the continents around? They showed that continents move apart and around the earth but really slowly. I think a few inches per year.

Kyle: Oh yeah. It was one big continent before. Then it split up.

Mother: And sometimes continents slip under each other or bump into each other. That can make ocean bottoms raise up and lose all their water. So people sometimes find shells even on mountains!

Kyle's parents used his scientific question to talk about several key ideas—geologic time, continental drift, and fossils—in this short conversation. The content, language, and cause-and-effect thinking that are nurtured in this conversation and others like it will help Kyle in language arts and science in kindergarten and later years of schooling.

SUMMARY

This chapter described how conversations can be used to cultivate eight key habits that children need to comprehend stories. It also provided practical strategies that you can use to frame and deepen your conversations about stories. Yet there are many more. You can do a little research on the topic of reading comprehension so you can add even more conversation strategies to your parenting toolkit.

BIBLIOGRAPHY

American Academy of Pediatrics, Committee on Public Education. "Media Education." *Pediatrics* 104, no. 2.1 (1999): 341–343.
Demi. *The Empty Pot*. New York: Square Fish Books, 1996.
DiCamillo, Kate. *Because of Winn-Dixie*. Somerville, MA: Candlewick Press, 2000.
Eastman, P. D. *Are You My Mother?* New York: Random House, 1960.
Hayes, Joe. *The Day It Snowed Tortillas*. El Paso, TX: Cinco Puntos Press, 2003.
Hughes, Langston. "Mother to Son" in *The Collected Poems of Langston Hughes*. London: Vintage Classics, 1995.
Lobell, Arnold. *Frog and Toad Are Friends*. New York: HarperCollins, 2003.
Munsch, Robert. *The Paper Bag Princess*. Toronto: Annick Press, 2018.
Pfister, Marcus. *The Rainbow Fish*. New York: NorthSouth Books, 1999.
Sachar, Louis. *Holes*. New York: Scholastic, 2000.
Wiesner, David. *Flotsam*. Boston: Clarion Books, 2006.

Chapter Four

Conversations about History

Conversations are tools for excavating and piecing together historical truths.

History spans from the early days of the universe to this very moment. It encompasses all the events, changes, ideas, actions, thoughts, and feelings of those who came before us—and of us. It includes how people chose to record the past and how we interpret it today. History, long ago and recent, has shaped all of us and will continue to do so.

So if you tend to talk about things that happened yesterday, last year, or a thousand years ago, you are already having conversations about history with your child. This chapter is focused on improving these conversations so that your child is more prepared for learning and talking about history in school and life.

Yet many parents still think history is boring. It conjures up memories of memorizing dates and names and reciting the causes of the Civil War. It brings up flashbacks of cramming for big history tests the night before, only to forget the information a few hours later. Unfortunately, this limited view of history, much of which comes from how history has been taught in school, turns many kids away from learning and talking about the past. Fortunately, there are many different parts of history that offer a smorgasbord of rich conversation opportunities.

REASONS TO CONVERSE ABOUT HISTORY WITH YOUR CHILD

Your Child Learns More History

One obvious benefit of history conversations is learning more history. The more your child thinks and talks about historical ideas in conversation, the better he or she understands and remembers them. Your child, for example, might be reading a story about the ancient Mayans. You ask basic questions about where they lived, what they ate, and so on. But you also prompt your child to think about their scientific achievements and the features of their civilization, perhaps comparing them to others, and possible causes of their decline, which is still a mystery. You even share your theory for the decline, along with your willingness to be persuaded to adopt a different theory.

And if your child (or you) asks, "Why is knowing history important?" here are several of the biggest reasons:

1. knowing history helps us understand the present and prepare for the future
2. knowing history helps us humans learn from successes and mistakes in the past—and ponder why we haven't learned from our mistakes
3. knowing history helps us know where we and others come from and why we are who we are
4. knowing history helps us to see how people can change the world

Conversations tend to clarify and "cement" ideas better in the brain than just reading or listening to them. This is especially important because children tend to live in the present. For many children, yesterday is as remote as a day in the Middle Ages. So what happened dozens or hundreds or thousands of years ago can use as much clarifying as possible in conversation. Here is a sample conversation.

Mother: So what did you learn from that show?

Jake: About the pyramids.

Mother: What about them?

Jake: They were big.

Mother: Where are they? Why were they built?

Jake: Egypt, I think. And they were castles for kings.

Mother: Yes, Egypt. It's in northern Africa. See? Here on the map. But they weren't castles; they were tombs, you know, where they buried kings.

Jake: They were big.

Your Child Develops Historical Thinking Skills

Conversations also allow your child to foster his or her historical thinking skills. As mentioned in the introduction, history has shaped, is shaping, and will shape your child. The better your child can think and talk about history, from many years ago or from this morning, the better prepared he or she will be for school and life.

Several thinking skills focused on in this chapter are:

- understanding causes and effects
- determining what is important in history
- empathizing and understanding different perspectives
- looking for bias in sources
- making and supporting claims about what happened in history

Conversations that include these skills are much juicier than just answering questions about dates and events. Take another look at the skills and consider how they can help your child not just in history classes but also in life. Notice the skills of identifying causes and effects, empathizing, and supporting claims in this conversation following a reading of *The Story of Ruby Bridges* (Coles, 2010).

Sara: Why'd they call Ruby names?

Father: Why do *you* think?

Sara: They didn't like her, maybe.

Father: They were racist and didn't want Ruby to go to their school.

Sara: What's racist?

Father: When you don't like people because of their skin color. Racists think they are better than people who are different from them.

Sara: That's bad. Ruby was a good person.

Father: Why?

Sara: She prayed for the racist people, the ones who yelled at her. And she forgives them. I don't know if I would do that.

Father: Me either. She is a good example for us.

Your Child Develops Language

A third benefit is language development. Your child hears history-based language that you use in conversation. Over time, terms that you use such as *led to*, *bias*, *caused*, *effects*, *motivation*, and so on tend to become more automatically understood and even used by your child in speech. As your child struggles (in a good way) to describe evolving historical ideas and thinking, he or she tries to use more complex language. Your child will use some of your language and the language of a text or TV show that you are discussing. You can encourage your child to try new words and expressions.

Notice in the following conversation how the father clarifies and models new language, which is then used by the child.

Father: What happened?

Matthew: There was a war.

Father: Who?

Matthew: The colonies and England.

Father: Why?

Matthew: I think they both wanted the land. And something about taxes.

Father: They didn't want to pay taxes?

Matthew: Yeah, but they wanted to vote in government, or something like that.

Father: I remember a phrase, no taxation without representation.

Matthew: Yeah, I heard that, but don't remember what it means.

Father: Representation means, like you said, to be able to vote for your interests, for what helps you in government. Like we have representatives for each state who are in Washington, D.C., and they supposedly vote for laws and ideas that help out each state. So the colonists?

Matthew: So the colonists got taxed, but they didn't get represented in England, and but they made lots of laws and stuff, and I think they kept doing taxes on them. So the colonists said, "No more"; then they did the Boston Tea Party.

GROWING YOUR CHILD'S HISTORICAL THINKING SKILLS

Conversations provide lots of great opportunities to develop children's historical thinking skills. The following skills are described separately here, but you will often use multiple skills in the same conversation.

Understanding Causes and Effects

Conversing about historical causes and effects builds your child's understandings of how history connects and flows. Throughout history, people have done things that caused other things to happen. Rulers started wars to expand their power, citizens rose up to fight for their freedom, explorers explored new lands to gain wealth and fame, inventors invented new ways to improve and destroy life, and so on.

One of the big reasons to talk about history is to know the mistakes of the past so that we don't repeat them. People must learn the causes of past mistakes, along with their unexpected effects, if we are to avoid making similar mistakes. Similarly, we need to learn about our past successes to pass this knowledge on and build on it for the future. All of this means that you should help your child to develop the skill of identifying causes and effects.

To identify causes and effects, it helps to know certain principles of causation in history. For example, when I hear about a war, I immediately think about what people often fight about: land, religion, and freedom, to name a few. Therefore, we can't really talk about causes and effects without some background knowledge of how things happen and what motivates people to do things. You and your child need to have some understanding of different types of social, political, physical, and psychological causes that tend to drive history.

Take a look at the following conversation and notice what the mother does to foster cause-and-effect thinking.

Robert: Can you help me with this question: "Why did people move west?"

Mother: That's a good question. Why do people move now?

Robert: Maybe to change jobs?

Mother: Yes, especially these days now, but there weren't jobs out west like today. What would they do?

Robert: Get gold maybe.

Mother: Yes, the Gold Rush motivated a lot of folks to head west. What else motivated them?

Robert: Maybe land? Like here it says they wanted freedom and open space.

Mother: So land and freedom? Freedom how?

Robert: I don't know. Maybe less rules and laws. Maybe they wanted to live in the Old West like the movies.

Mother: Only it was the "New West" back then, right?

Robert: I guess.

Notice how the mother pushed Robert to answer his own questions and how she used a key cause-and-effect term, *motivated*, to help Robert think about how people in the past were feeling. Over time, even short conversations like this one can build important historical thinking skills and language in children.

Here are some strategies for conversing about causes and effects in history.

1. Model the cause-and-effect questions that you ask yourself as you think about history topics. Then model your thinking as you try to answer the questions. Model the language (and write it somewhere) that you use to process your answers. For example, ask questions such as "Why did the Pilgrims leave England?" or "What were the effects of French Revolution?"
2. Think out loud to describe how to come up with possible causes and effects to answer the questions in the first strategy. Most causes in history fall under the categories of fear, racism, religion, compassion, lust for wealth, lust for power, lust for fame, desire for knowledge, desire for freedom, desire for truth, and natural events.
3. Use diagrams, time lines, or other visuals to help your child see and remember causes and effects of something in history. Some visuals and related activities are included later in this chapter.

As children develop this skill, they gradually achieve one of the main purposes of knowing history: *learning where we came from and who we are and reflecting on who we might become.*

Cause-Effect Visual

For those of you who like visual aids and going a little deeper into causes and effects with your child, you can use a visual like this one (figure 4.1). Not coincidentally, many history teachers use similar visuals. This type of organizer allows you and your child to see and talk about the multiple causes and effects of something that happened. It also asks you to converse about how much influence the causes might have had and how important its effects were.

1. Pick an event or condition such as the Boston Tea Party, building of the Great Wall in China, democracy, or something else that your child just learned or read about and put it in the center oval.
2. Talk about possible causes for the event. Then pick the top three to put in the left hand arrows (e.g., taxation without representation, angry at lack of freedom from England, English people would get mad because they like tea).
3. Converse about how much you both think each cause influenced the event and why. Put an X on the dotted lines to indicate how strong or weak you think the influence was.
4. Talk about probable effects of the event or condition. These can be other events or effects on people involved or related to the future. Put the top three in the effects boxes on the right (e.g., British closed Boston Harbor, passed Intolerable Acts, sparked American Revolution).

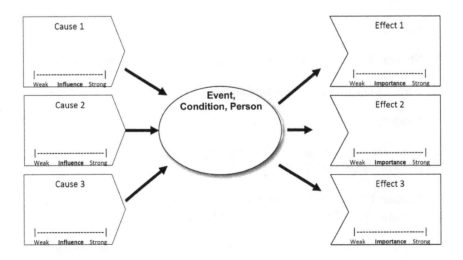

Figure 4.1. Cause-Effect Visual Organizer

5. Talk about how much importance each effect had in history, and put an X along the dotted line between strong and weak. Come up with reasons and evidence for this rating.

Here is a sample conversation between a mother and her nine-year-old son, Alex. His mother decided to ask him about history and to use the cause-effect visual.

Mother: What did you learn at history today?

Alex: About Columbus.

Mother: What about him?

Alex: He discovered America.

Mother: Yes, he's famous for that, but he wasn't the first person here, was he?

Alex: People were already here.

Mother: How about we put Columbus's arrival into these cause and effect boxes and see what we get? You know, for fun.

Alex: OK. Not sure how *fun* it'll be, but OK.

Mother: So, we put "Columbus lands in the Caribbean in 1492" in the middle.

Alex: OK.

Mother: What's one cause of that? What motivated him and his sailors?

Alex: I think one cause was find an easier way to get to India, for spices.

Mother: Why did they want that?

Alex: They didn't want to go all the way around Africa. It was dangerous and expensive, I think.

Mother: OK. I'll put that as Cause 1. I think another cause was that he was greedy. I think he wanted to be famous and get rich.

Alex: Yeah, we read something he wrote to the king about giving them gold and slaves.

Mother: Yeah. OK. One more cause?

Alex: Maybe religion?

Mother: How so?

Alex: Well, we saw a painting of Columbus's landing and it had people with crosses.

Mother: Do you think the painter was accurate?

Alex: No, but I also think we read that they wanted to turn people to Christians.

Mother: How strong were these causes? Like finding a way to India?

Alex: Maybe medium.

Mother: Why?

Alex: I don't think he really wanted to find a new route just to like improve the world. I think it was he was greedy, like the second one here.

Mother: So you think the second cause is stronger?

Alex: Yeah. I'd put that high because of what he wrote and all the bad things he did, like turning people into slaves.

Mother: And I think the religion one is medium, too. Maybe even low because I think for a lot of the Europeans, it was an excuse to take over and take their resources. Now what?

Alex: The effects. One effect was turning the people into slaves and giving them diseases that killed a lot of them.

Mother: That's a huge effect. A negative one, right?

Alex: Yeah. And another is the new things that each side of the ocean got, like traded.

Mother: Like what did they trade?

Alex: Horses, pigs, sugar, and cotton . . . and chocolate.

Mother: And how important was the trading of those things?

Alex: I think a lot because it got a lot more explorers to come.

Mother: What do you mean?

Alex: Well, they wanted more and more sugar and chocolate, so more people came to get it. And they . . . they moved here and took over the land.

Mother: So that's another big effect, right?

Because they used the diagram, this conversation was more structured and school-like than most conversations at home. But you can see how the diagram can be helpful to deepen a child's building of historical ideas. Notice the mother, more than once, asks for clarification and support and pushes for thinking about causes and effects. And the conversation was likely a lot longer than if they hadn't used the diagram.

Determining Historical Importance

A "companion skill" for understanding causes and effects is determining historical importance. This means thinking and talking about how important a person, event, or condition was. Importance usually depends on the long-term impact of its effects. The larger "book-worthy" events usually bring about major social, economic, or political changes. These often include wars, human migrations, rises and falls of empires, and technological revolutions. For example, the two world wars are important because of the widespread and drastic changes they caused.

When it comes to learning history in school, some people at some point decided which historical facts, ideas, and people should be in the books and lessons. But you and your child have more choice. What should you choose? In this chapter, there are wide ranges of topics, and there are thousands more out there. You can choose based on various criteria: what interests you and your child, events or people that connect to your family or geographic location, current books and TV programs, trips to different places with interesting histories, and so on.

You can ask several questions to get you going, such as:

- Is this important? Why?
- What resulted from it?
- If this hadn't happened, how would history be different?
- Could it happen again? Why?

Here's an example. Eleven-year-old Elena and her father were talking about the meaning of democracy and who should be allowed to vote. Look for how the focus on importance in general moves into its importance to the child.

Father: What did you learn in school today?

Elena: Nothing.

Father: What about in social studies? I saw you work on that drawing of democracy yesterday.

Elena: We're still on that.

Father: So what is democracy?

Elena: People vote.

Father: Why is that important?

Elena: I don't know.

Father: What would happen if you don't have democracy?

Elena: Maybe you get bad people as leaders.

Father: So that's important because . . . ?

Elena: 'Cause bad leaders make everyone mad. Maybe they'll fight, like a revolution.

Father: Hmmm, yeah. So is democracy important to you?

Elena: Not really. I can't vote. I'm not old enough.

Father: Should you be able to?

Elena: Maybe.

Father: The results affect you, too. Sometimes even more.

Elena: We don't know the stuff. You know, to vote on it.

Father: What could you and your friends do to be able to vote?

Elena: I don't know. Vote on it? But we won't win 'cause we can't vote.

Father: You never know. You could look into how to change the voting age. Laws are changing every year.

Historical Empathizing and Seeing Multiple Perspectives

Empathy means stepping into another person's shoes to think and feel as they do. Empathy helps your child better understand others' experiences and thoughts. But there is a big challenge when it comes to empathizing with people in the past. We must constantly battle our self-focused tendencies to perceive life as we have experienced it.

We all (including our children) must strive to be humble and open-minded when we set out to walk in another person's shoes, whether they lived three thousand years ago or were just on the news this morning. Many influences have bombarded you and your child since birth, such as TV, school, movies, music, trips, family, and friends. All of these work together to influence how you and your child empathize.

In order to empathize with someone, you need to learn as much as you can about the person or group of people. What were the details of the person's childhood, relationships, goals, actions, words, failures, and successes? How did these life factors affect this person's personality and actions? You then try to filter out your thoughts and feelings that bias your perceptions of the other person. Then you generate a likely set of thoughts and feelings of the other person(s).

In the conversations that build and depend on empathy, it helps to ask lots of questions. Here are several examples of these questions.

- What do you think she was feeling when that happened?
- Why do you think she would . . . ?
- What do you think those words meant back then?
- What did freedom mean to people back then?
- Why do you think he/she did that?
- If you were in his/her shoes, what would you have done? Why?
- If you had to write a journal entry from the perspective of (person), what would you put in it?
- How do you think they felt?

Notice how the father in the following sample conversation helps Rosario step into the shoes of others who are very different from her.

Father: What did you learn about in school today?

Rosario: The Spanish made war with Aztecs and beat them.

Father: How do you think the Aztecs felt when the Spanish conquered them?

Rosario: Bad.

Father: Imagine you were in their shoes, like an Aztec.

Rosario: But I don't want to be one.

Father: Just imagine you are; it helps. And you have your life, just working away, and then boom, these strangers come in.

Rosario: I don't like it. It's not fair. It's our land and pyramids. We built them. And they just want gold.

Father: So what do you do?

Rosario: I don't know, maybe fight back?

Father: So why didn't they all fight back? There were a lot more Aztecs than Spanish soldiers. They could have beat them quickly.

Rosario: Something about gods, maybe, like they were afraid.

The father used several helpful prompts to get Rosario thinking from the perspective of an Aztec. Even though this wasn't a particularly profound conversation, it got some good thinking going. And many conversations like this one over time will have a profound effect on her.

Looking for Bias in Sources

Not that you want your child to be skeptical about everything, but a healthy dose of wariness is helpful when it comes to past and present sources of information. Especially these days when a lot of news (a.k.a. recent history) and other "facts" are easily accessible and fudgeable online, children need to be able to look for biases in sources. They need to remember that many people write things with ulterior motives in mind—often to sell you a product or convince you to think a certain way. Conversations about the "truth strength" of what your child reads and hears can be very helpful throughout life. Children need to know that lots of people out there exaggerate, bend the truth, and lie.

People who are good at looking for bias tend to ask the following questions, which you can model in your conversations with your child. You would, of course, reword some of them depending on the age of your child.

- What is the purpose of the story, article, or movie?
- Does it exaggerate or lie about anything?
- How does the idea that "history is written by the winners" apply here?
- Did the author (or speaker or producer) have any reason to not be exactly true to what happened?
- Was/is the author qualified to write on the topic?
- Does she or he have any biases or agendas that might affect the writing?
- Will the author (or producer) gain, monetarily or otherwise, from this text?
- Does the author state opinions, stereotype, or generalize?
- Does he/she use overly strong words such as *ridiculous*, *crazy*, *insane*, *worthless*, *pathetic*, *ideal*, *obvious*, *clearly*, and so on?
- Does the author fairly present and then address counter opinions and counterevidence?
- Are credible supporting examples or data given? Are their sources cited?
- Are the conclusions supported by the evidence/facts?
- Could there be other factors or variables that influenced the outcome?

By having lots of conversations in which these types of questions come up, your child will eventually ask them too. And such questions will help your child think much more deeply about history in school and beyond.

Here is a sample conversation. Notice how the mother nudges Aaron toward thinking about how different sources can be biased, including textbooks used in school.

Mother: What did you learn in history class today?

Aaron: About Columbus discovering America.

Mother: Interesting. Did he really discover it?

Aaron: No, but he's famous for it.

Mother: Why do you think that? I read that he did a lot of bad things like taking slaves and hurting people he met.

Aaron: He wanted to . . . to be famous, maybe, and rich?

Mother: Probably.

Aaron: So why doesn't our history book put those bad things about him?

Mother: I don't know. Should they?

Aaron: Yes, we should learn that he . . . he wasn't a hero.

Mother: We could read what the first people there thought, but I don't think they wrote much down, and I'm not sure the Europeans would have let much of what they wrote down survive anyway.

Aaron: Why?

Mother: Why do you think?

Aaron: Maybe 'cause they did lots of bad things.

Making, Supporting, and Comparing Historical Arguments

This is the skill that historians are best known for. Historians seldom take history tests or regurgitate the ideas of others. They instead make new claims about history or they find new support for existing claims. A claim is an important idea or argument about a historical issue, event, person, and so forth. It is an idea that is not obvious, not a proven fact, and needs to be supported with evidence. Several interesting historical claims are:

- In 1421, China landed on both the west and east coasts of North America.
- The patriots were rebels who worked hard to convince other colonists to rebel against England.
- The United States should not have entered the Vietnam War.
- Columbus did not discover America.
- States should be able to secede from the United States.
- The United States is not a true democracy.

Notice how claims like these tend to spark interest in talking about them with others. They don't just involve memorizing information or responding with "Hmmm. That's an interesting fact." When you make a claim or counterclaim, you need to support it with evidence, just like you would support any argument in life. If, for example, your child claims that she doesn't think Columbus discovered America, ask her for some evidence and ask her to question the value of her sources.

When there are two claims that conflict or "compete," congratulations! You now have a juicy historical argument, which usually fosters rich conversation. You both clarify and support both ideas in order to build them up as much as possible, and then you compare the two to see which side's evidence is stronger or heavier.

Be careful not to immediately pick one side and start debating right away. Instead, collaborate to build up both sides and then objectively evaluate the weight of evidence for each. You and your child might decide that different evidences have different weights. This is okay, as long as you both talk about it. Here is an example:

Mother: Tyler, do you think Sacagawea should have helped Lewis and Clark?

Tyler: I don't know. I don't think she had a choice.

Mother: What do you mean?

Tyler: She was married to a guy who was hired to help them. Lewis and Clark found out she spoke a language they needed. She was going to have a baby; I don't think she wanted to go.

Mother: So she should have refused?

Tyler: Well, it wasn't good for her or the baby. But she might have saved their lives.

Mother: How so?

Tyler: She knew one of the tribes and told them not to fight with Lewis and Clark. I think the chief was her brother or something.

Mother: So she probably saved their lives, and she helped them succeed in their expedition. But was it good that they succeeded, for everyone?

Tyler: What do you mean?

Mother: Well, after that, people moved into those areas to take over the land. And a lot of Native Americans lived there already. There were fights, and they were asked to move to reservations. We don't have much history written down from their point of view.

Tyler: So for Native Americans it was bad? Maybe Sacagawea shouldn't have helped them. It might have been better for her and her baby and her people.

Mother: Maybe. It's a good question, isn't it?

Notice how the mother helped Tyler to develop not only some history knowledge but also the big idea that a lot of history, especially of certain groups of people, wasn't written down. She also focused on the skills of supporting a claim, clarifying ideas, and even understanding causes and effects.

HISTORY TOPICS AND HOW TO CONVERSE ABOUT THEM

Most people have not had enough exposure to *interesting* history topics. A handful are mentioned in this chapter, but more are found in the following resources:

- magazines such as *Smithsonian, National Geographic,* and *Time for Kids*
- TV shows such as those on the History Channel and PBS, movies about historical events and people, historical fiction stories
- online articles on websites such as https://www.historyforkids.net, https://www.ducksters.com/history, and news sites that focus on current events and commentary

It helps to "try out" different history topics that might interest your child. You can start with topics that you know about. But often you will have to do some extra snooping around to find the history that is juicy enough to hold your child's interest. Here are some categories and topics to try out.

Conversing about Events

Events are the most common type of topic that you will tend to talk about. You can talk about their causes and effects, as well as the interesting people and details involved in events. For example, in the following conversation, notice the focus on the event, but also look for other historical thinking skills and conversation skills.

Mother: So why was the Boston Tea Party so important? All they did was dump some tea into the harbor, right?

Carla: I think it was to show the English they were tired of paying taxes.

Mother: But taxes weren't that expensive, right?

Carla: Maybe they were mad the British would just decide to tax them, like whenever they wanted.

Mother: What do you mean?

Carla: Something about taxation and no representing. I don't know.

Mother: Oh. So the British government didn't have any people in it to represent what the colonies wanted.

Carla: Well, they didn't want taxes.

Mother: So did the Tea Party work?

Carla: Well, I think so. It was famous.

Mother: But why was it so famous?

Carla: I think 'cause it was the first thing they did to fight back and to be like rebels. And it got the British super mad, so they closed the harbor.

Mother: And I bet that made the colonists even more angry. Angry enough for a revolution.

Here are additional examples of conversation-fostering questions that focus on major events. If you have the time, notice which historical thinking skills are prompted by the different questions.

- What was the Bronze Age? Why was it important?
- What was the Agricultural Revolution? Why was it important?
- Would you have taken part in the Gold Rush? Why or why not?
- How did cities get started? How are cities helpful?
- How did European colonization (of Africa, India, Americas) change the world? How did it change the lives of people already living in those places?
- How did the American Civil War change the United States and its people?
- What caused World War II? What were its effects?
- Why did Americans move west in the 1800s?
- Did Chinese ships map much of the world seventy years before Columbus crossed the Atlantic? Did he use any of those maps?

Conversing about People

Conversations can also be about people, famous or not. Most famous people do things to make major changes in history. There is usually a large amount of information on these people such as how they grew up, things they said and wrote, and what motivated them to do what they did. Many have traits and values that make them role models.

There are people, for example, who endured hardship when they stood up to unjust laws and treatment (e.g., Gandhi, Martin Luther King Jr., Harriet Tubman). There are many other less famous people who endured worse. And there are the people who are the opposite of role models. You can have conversations about whether or not historical people should be heroes (e.g., Columbus), if we should try to be like them or not, and how they should be described in history texts.

Here are several conversation-worthy questions focused on famous people in history:

- Would you have risked your life to help Harriet Tubman in her work?
- How did Lewis and Clark survive their two-year expedition?
- Why didn't Martin Luther King Jr. use violence to fight against racism?
- Was Rosa Parks a hero? Why?

Before the following conversation, Sara's father had seen her reading a short description of Columbus Day. He then did a little research on Columbus. Notice the focus on getting to the historical truth, recognizing bias, and clarifying some of the ideas about a famous person.

Father: What's that book about?

Sara: Christopher Columbus.

Father: What about him?

Sara: He discovered America.

Father: He is famous for that, but I think others got here before him.

Sara: Like who?

Father: Leif Erickson, a Viking, landed in what is now North America around five hundred years before Columbus. And I think I remember reading that Columbus was met by someone on the island who spoke Portuguese.

Sara: So they should be famous for discovering it, right?

Father: Maybe for being the first Europeans to visit the Americas. But what about the people who were already here?

Sara: You mean the Native Americans?

Father: Yeah.

Sara: They got here way before Columbus and those others. Why aren't they famous for discovering North America?

Father: Good question. What do you think?

Sara: I think that . . . I don't know.

Famous people get a lot of ink in history books, but it is equally—or perhaps even more—important to learn about how non-famous people thought, felt, and lived. There were (and still are) a lot more average folks, after all. What did groups of people believe, fear, hope for, work toward, and do each day? These and similar questions can foster interesting conversations and learning about entire groups of people and how to understand them and their contributions to history and to humanity.

Here are several conversation-worthy questions focused on how groups of people lived:

- How did the average Greek merchant, Roman servant, Qing Dynasty farmer, Egyptian slave, Mayan artist, or Wampanoag child live? What did they do? How did they think and feel? What goals did they have?
- What made the ancient Greeks (or Romans, Aztecs, Egyptians, Aksumites, Incas, Anasazi, Mesopotamians, Persians, etc.) unique? How did they contribute to human history?
- How did the group of people entertain themselves?
- How did they grow and prepare food?
- What religious beliefs did they have? Why did they believe and have certain practices?
- What positive things did the group give to future people like us (art, inventions, ideas, foods, etc.)?
- How were they similar and different to us?

Artifacts, Art, and Inventions

One of the primary ways to learn about people in history is looking at what they left behind. In general, the further into the past you go, the less information we have about the people. For our more distant ancestors, we tend to rely on things that have been dug up by archaeologists.

Artifacts tend to include pots, religious objects, images, scrolls, writings, burial objects, money, toys, and musical instruments. Art includes sculptures, paintings, buildings, decorations, and works of literature. Inventions include tools, machines, weapons, musical instruments, and other things for making life easier. All of these are, in a sense, puzzle pieces that we put together to form a picture of how people thought and lived. As you can imagine, some juicy conversations can result from putting these pieces together.

Here are several conversation-worthy questions focused on artifacts, art, and inventions:

- What was this object used for? Why didn't they use something else?
- How was this used?

- Based on objects like this, why do archaeologists think that the people ___?
- How did this invention (wheel, car, Internet, plane, telephone, printing press, television, rockets, computer, electricity) improve life for people?
- Was this invention (e.g., plane, car, computer, cell phone) good overall for people? How might it be bad?

Mysteries and Questions

Historical mysteries and questions can make for very interesting conversations. The artifacts, records, and clues that would clearly answer them don't exist. We therefore need to make educated guesses that are supported by any pieces of evidence that we do have combined with historical interpretations, inferences, and reasoning.

Here are several conversation-worthy questions focused on historical mysteries and questions:

- Why did the Mayan civilization decline?
- What happened to the colony at Roanoke?
- Who created the Sphinx and why?
- Who was the legend of King Arthur based on?
- Who, if anyone, made the Bimini Road? Why?
- Did the lost city of Atlantis exist?
- Who made the thirteen crystal skulls found in South America?
- What was in the one million scrolls in the Library of Alexandria before it burned down?
- Was Robin Hood based on a real person? Why was he so popular?

There are many more than these, and some interesting ones can come from books and movies that you come across. And movies, in particular, offer chances to also talk about heavy biases and embellishments often used by their creators to make money.

Big Ideas in History

It can help you to have in mind several big ideas and major themes that guide the thinking of historians and others who like to converse about history. Here are some examples:

- If we don't learn from past mistakes, we are doomed to repeat them.
- We can try to understand the people of the past, but we can only partially do so because we are much more different from them than we think we are.

- Most historical sources—and the people who interpret them—are biased in some way.
- Technology often makes big positive and negative differences.
- "History is written by the winners." Most history, especially that of billions of poor and powerless people, was never recorded.
- When farmers had extra food, they could trade it for goods that others made. This made other jobs, towns, cities, and civilizations possible.
- Geography shapes culture.
- Common causes in history fit under the categories of greed, hunger for power and control, desire for freedom from oppression and injustice, desire to discover new lands and scientific breakthroughs, natural disasters, and religion.
- History is not just black and white, heroes and villains; it contains the complexity of people and politics, not just easy x versus y. Were some "great leaders" worse humans than the average person?

Notice how the mother brings up some of these big ideas in the following conversation about the decline of the Mayan civilization over a thousand years ago. They had just read a short nonfiction book on the civilization that ended by saying that scholars still don't know for sure why it declined.

Mother: Why do you think their civilization declined?

Amaira: I don't know. Maybe they ran out of food?

Mother: But they had farms.

Amaira: Maybe there were too many people for it.

Mother: Yes, civilizations have lots of people. Not all of them are farmers. Why?

Amaira: 'Cause farmers grow extra food and sell it. That was in the book.

Mother: But then what if there was drought, too?

Amaira: What's that?

Mother: It doesn't rain for months or years. If there's no good irrigation, crops die.

Amaira: Then no food for anyone.

Mother: Yes, so that would make everyone go back to looking for food, right? No one to run the temples or be in government or fight against invaders. Hmmm.

Amaira: So maybe too many people and maybe a drought.

Mother: Yes, and do you think that could happen to us? What were their mistakes that we can learn from?

Amaira: They didn't grow enough food, and crops died. Maybe like they needed to save more water for the plants they ate.

Mother: So irrigation technology would have helped?

Amaira: Yeah.

Idea-Building Visual

You can partially fill in this visual organizer (figure 4.2) before your conversation and then add to it after the conversation with your child. You can use it to show your child the process of co–building up a meaningful idea in conversation. In the top bar, you put the big idea or claim that you are building up. In the bricks, you include things that are helpful for building up the idea, such as questions and definitions. In most of the bricks, you will put supporting examples and clarifications, the main two ways to build up ideas. What you put into the bricks will tend to come from books, videos, websites,

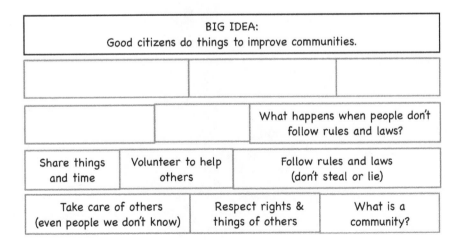

Figure 4.2. Idea-Building Visual

conversations with others, and life experiences. The big ideas can build up over time, even a lifetime. Good conversations can play large roles in this building.

SUMMARY

You can and should have powerful conversations about history with your child. Whether it is ancient or recent history, dig into as many topics as possible and try to hone some of the skills described in this chapter during your conversations. If your child is in school, find out what history or social studies topics are being taught this year. Try out different topics and keep an eye open for topics that come from stories and other texts that you read to your child.

BIBLIOGRAPHY

Coles, Robert. *The Story of Ruby Bridges.* St. Louis, MO: Turtleback Books, 2010.

Chapter Five

Conversations about Science

Walk and talk in all-out wonder.

Some of the most interesting conversations in the universe are about how it works. You might look at the moon and wonder how it got there or what would happen if it weren't there. Your child might watch a feather fall and wonder why it falls more slowly than a rock. You both might be on a walk and wonder why the leaves change color, how a heavy plane flies, or what makes the sparks in a sweater coming out of the dryer. These and many more wonderings can be topics of rich and productive science conversations with your child.

This chapter offers ideas for helping your child do well in science in school, but conversations about science will also help your child succeed beyond school. Your science conversations will most directly help your child in science classes and science-related professions. Yet most jobs require different degrees of scientific thinking and knowledge. For example, in many jobs, workers try to maximize production and/or profits by figuring out the optimal combination of variables. They try different things, analyze results, and make changes.

Science conversations tend to have two major purposes: deepening an understanding and/or solving a problem. These can overlap of course. For the first type, you might have conversations with your child about space exploration, bird migration, blood circulation, water boiling, combustion engines, gravity, insect classification, the reasons for seasons, and so on. For the second type, you might talk about solving science-related problems such as malaria, tornadoes, pollution, hunger, earthquakes, poverty, asteroids, living on the moon, deforestation, bringing back extinct species, and so forth.

Science in school is typically divided into several types of courses:

- physics, which includes topics such as gravity, forces, electricity, magnetism, elements, atoms, molecules, chemistry, etc.
- biology, which includes plants, animals, human body, cells, adaptation, health, etc.
- earth and space, which includes weather, geology, planets and stars, plate tectonics, oceans, erosion, etc.
- social, which includes psychology, communication, economics, sociology, anthropology, etc.

Being familiar with these branches of science will help you to notice opportunities to talk with your child as topics come up. These topics might pop up from what you are doing at home (cooking, playing) or out in nature (e.g., hiking, swimming), what you are watching on TV (e.g., nature shows, cartoons that defy the laws of physics), or your child's science homework (e.g., doing an experiment, reading the text and answering questions). Be ready to talk about science, ask questions, and encourage your child to ask questions—especially questions that begin with *why* and *how*.

There are many science topics to talk about. A few topics that might interest you and your child include clean energy from ocean waves, electric cars, black holes, life next to ocean thermal vents, space travel, genetic engineering, life on other planets, and alternate universes. You can also do little nature walks, discovery labs, and experiments at home. Do a little fun reading about potential topics to help prepare you for conversations with your child. You can also be looking for topics that pop up as you observe the world, watch science-related programs, watch the news, read articles, and help your child with science homework.

Your child may not become a scientist per se in the future, but a strong understanding of how things work, as well as knowing how to figure out how things work by talking with others, can benefit your child a lot in school and life. The rest of this chapter helps you think more deeply about how conversations with your child can nourish and strengthen this potential.

BENEFITS OF TALKING ABOUT SCIENCE WITH YOUR CHILD

Your Child Learns and Remembers More Science

When your child describes or explains something to you, this helps him or her to remember it better. And when you explain ideas to your child in a conversation, he or she tends to learn and remember them. If there is some "clashing" between your child's originally held misconceptions about science and new facts that you introduce, then even more learning happens. For example, your child might explain that she saw the moon this evening and it was a different shape than three days ago. She says, "It's weird the moon changes its shape. It's round and then like half round. Where does the other half go?" You then explain, perhaps with the help of a ball and flashlight, what happens. You might even go on to say that you wonder why one side of the moon is always dark and talk about possible hypotheses.

Your Child Builds Science Thinking Skills

Conversations also allow you to both model and help your child to practice thinking skills needed in science. These skills include identifying causes and effects, analyzing variables, experimenting, interpreting, and applying. For example, encouraging your child to keep asking "why" (though some children do this automatically) can help your child to keep drilling down into root causes of scientific phenomena. Eventually, the root causes can become too advanced for you or your child, but the thinking skill gets stronger.

Your Child Develops Science Language

Conversations are rich soil for developing the language of science. Just like other areas of learning (history, math, literature), science has unique ways of using language to describe its concepts. As you describe scientific ideas in conversation, you model how to use scientific language for your child. And your child, in turn, uses some of the language that you model to describe his or her thoughts, thereby practicing the use of scientific language.

Science language is much more than a set of big science words. It also includes using words that are commonly used outside of science in a variety of sentences to describe:

- science situations and questions
- theories and hypotheses
- ways to design and perform effective experiments
- interpretations and explanations of evidence
- ways to apply new ideas and solve problems

Conversations give your child much-needed practice in using language to do these things. For example, notice the language used in the conversation below about the water cycle. Notice how the conversation likely maintains Trish's interest in the topic and communicating about it. And think about the learning that might not happen if Trish had just listened to her father (or a teacher) "lecture" on the topic.

Trish: It's raining.

Father: Why do you think it rains?

Trish: Clouds are crying, maybe?

Father: I like that hypothesis. But do clouds have eyes that cry? Let's look at them.

Trish: I don't see any eyes, so I don't know why.

Father: Actually, clouds get heavy with water vapor and finally the vapor condenses into drops of rain and falls.

Trish: Huh?

Father: First, water evaporates, turns into vapor, like when a puddle dries up in the sun. There's water vapor right now in this air, but we can't see it. It is like really tiny drops of water that float in the air. Then condense means that they come together into bigger drops and get heavy enough to fall. So if someone asks you, what is rain?

Trish: It's when water vapor comes from water; it dries up. Then it condense . . . condenses into big drops and then falls from clouds.

Father: And then?

Trish: Then rain makes puddles and dries up again.

Father: Yeah, it also makes rivers that go into lakes and oceans. And that's the water cycle. It keeps on going year after year. It's so interesting that one drop of water keeps evaporating up into the sky and then falling down as rain millions of times!

Your Child Gets More Interested in Science

Conversations can make scientific ideas and skills more interesting for your child. One of the best ways to understand something is to talk with someone (e.g., you) who can explain it, answer questions, and help children clarify their ideas. And when your child better understands something, he or she will more likely be interested in it. You should also show *your* interest and wonder during conversations, as the father did in the previous conversation. You can clarify ideas and help your child come up with his or her own questions, experiments, and concepts to explore. You can also help build up your child's science language and experiences so that he or she can be more confident when participating in science lessons at school.

GROWING YOUR CHILD'S SCIENCE SKILLS THROUGH CONVERSATION

The following skills are described separately in this section, but all can happen in one conversation, as you will see in the conversation samples in this chapter. Most of these skills tend to be included in what is loosely called the "scientific method." Your child may or may not pursue a career in science, but he or she can develop these vital scientific (and life) skills through frequent conversations with you.

Observing

Observation is the foundation of science. Each observation is a potential "brick" for building good questions, hypotheses, and conclusions. For example, your child might observe steam disappear as water boils, look at the moon through a telescope, find creatures at low tide, watch a TV show about volcanoes, and so on. Think of all the questions that can emerge from such observations. And for you, this means sharing your own observations and questions and always being ready for chances to prompt your child to observe and ponder in scientific ways.

A lot of observation can also happen in "hands-on science activities." For example, your child might follow a science procedure with each step described or shown in a drawing. These are common in science lessons at school, but many can and should also happen at home. Just look up home experimentation ideas on the Internet. For example, you and your child might follow steps to build a model that shows how solar and lunar eclipses happen.

You might have your child make observations while building a windmill, making a model electric car, growing plants from seeds, making baking soda rockets, or similar activities. It is tempting for you to get caught up in the fun, so don't forget to encourage your child to observe and share his or her observations as much as possible. Some parents will even present observation challenges, such as "Let's see if you can come up with ten observations while you watch a candle burn."

Here is a sample conversation focused on observation as Brenda and her mother were walking home from school in the fall.

Mother: What do you notice?

Brenda: What do you mean?

Mother: What do you see that's interesting? Maybe in the trees or sky?

Brenda: The trees are different.

Mother: How?

Brenda: Some lose . . . lost the leaves and others are green still.

Mother: Great observation! The ones with little needles, like fir trees, stay green. They're called evergreen trees. The others with leaves lose them for the winter.

Brenda: But why?

Notice how asking Brenda to notice something interesting led to some extra learning about trees and to a great question about why some trees are different and why trees lose their leaves. The more you can get your child to ask rich questions, the more engaged they will be in conversations about the topic.

Generating Good Questions

After observing something, you can encourage children to ask questions that start with *why* (e.g., Why does more water cause more growth? Why do grasshoppers jump? Why is the sun warm? Why do we never see one side of the moon?); *how* (e.g., How do mountains form? How do bats find food?); and *if* (e.g., If I give more water to the plants, will more tomatoes grow? If we dig straight down for miles and miles, what will we find?).

Given that many children tend to have plenty of questions anyway, you might not need to be that concerned about their quantity. But often we can help them add some juicier, more conversation-worthy questions to their arsenal. There are three broad types of juicy science questions:

1. questions that can be answered with hands-on experiments (e.g., Which materials stick to magnets?) and discovery labs (e.g., What happens when you insert a bar of soap into water with pepper in it?)
2. questions that have solid answers in textbooks and other sources (Why is the sky blue? Why are there tides?)
3. questions that aren't 100 percent answerable (Is there life on other planets? Should we bring back extinct species?)

In your conversations, try out all three of these types of questions and encourage your child to ask them as well. Many questions will stem from observation, and they will usually ask for an explanation of what was observed: "Why doesn't the moon fall?" "How does the cut on my finger heal?" "Which batteries last the longest?" A question could also be more open-ended like "Can we come up with a pill to prevent the common cold?" When a question comes up that lends itself to a doable lab or mini-experiment, jump on the chance. Then converse with your child to build up the details and answers together.

Hypothesizing

In order to build strong answers to their questions, children need to hypothesize possible and probable answers. A hypothesis is an educated guess, or likely idea, that might answer the question. For example, a child might hypothesize: "the moon doesn't fall because it's full of helium"; "my cut heals because it dries up"; "D batteries last the longest"; "flowers are baby trees"; "giving lots of water every day will grow more tomatoes." Notice that most hypotheses are based on some logic and previous knowledge. The child knew that helium is a gas that is lighter than air, that cuts dry up, that there are different sizes of batteries, that both flowers and trees are plants, and that tomatoes need a certain amount of water to grow. Children's brains were designed to make connections and hypotheses like these all day long.

Conversations can encourage and improve hypothesizing skills. You can ask your child what he or she thinks will happen, why, or why something happened. If your child gets "stuck," you can bring up knowledge and experiences that might help your child come up with logical hypotheses. For example, notice in the conversation below how the father does this.

Father: What do you think will happen to your heart when you run really fast?

Ivan: I don't know.

Father: Make a guess.

Ivan: Maybe it will go faster.

Father: Interesting. Why do you think that?

Ivan: 'Cause I'm running fast?

Father: Yes. Your muscles get tired, right? And what do they need?

Ivan: Ice cream?

Father: Ha ha, but yes, that's food, and they need it, too. But they also need oxygen that's in the air. That's why you need to breathe faster, too. But how does the oxygen get from your lungs to your muscles?

Ivan: My heart?

Father: Yes, your heart pumps faster when you run faster, to have the blood carry oxygen to your muscle's cells.

Experimenting

An experiment involves doing something to test a hypothesis. For example, when a child who is taking a bath hypothesizes that a thing has to have air in it in order to float, his father might ask him to come up with an experiment to test this hypothesis.

Experimenting involves testing to see if the real world does what the hypothesis predicts. Usually the hypothesis predicts that the change in a certain variable (e.g., a type of object in the tub) will have a certain effect (float or not). Most experiments try to keep all variables constant but one. If you don't, you don't know if the change in your hypothesized variable made a difference.

What is called the "independent variable" is the one you change, and the "dependent variable" is the thing that you observe or measure—the dependent variable depends on the independent variable. The experiment then strengthens or weakens the hypothesis by saying that the independent variable influences the dependent variable.

Let's look at an example. For the hypothesis in the following conversation, the child decided to give a different amount of water to the plants. Water is the independent variable, and plant growth is the dependent variable. If the most-watered plant yields the most tomatoes, Melissa's hypothesis is stronger (but not necessarily true for all time and all plants).

Mother: What do you want to know about the tomato plants?

Melissa: If more water makes more tomatoes.

Mother: How can you find out?

Melissa: The Internet?

Mother: Well, the Internet might give you a general idea, but you want to know about these plants in your garden. That's not on the Internet. How else?

Melissa: I could experiment, like we did with the potatoes and the light.

Mother: OK. Try that, but with water this time, right? What's your scientific question?

Melissa: How much water for the most tomatoes?

Mother: OK. What do you think will happen?

Melissa: I think more water will make more tomatoes.

Mother: OK. So what's the experiment?

Melissa: I put more water on the plants.

Mother: But will you be able to compare more water versus less water if all the plants get the same amount?

Melissa: Um, then I can give plants different water.

Mother: Each day, right? And what all needs to be the same, except for the water? What else makes tomatoes grow?

Melissa: The sun.

Mother: So do all the plants in your experiment get the same amount of light?

Melissa: Yeah, I guess.

Mother: What else?

Melissa: Ground, fertilizer, type of tomato?

Mother: What would happen if you gave different amounts of fertilizer and different amounts of water?

Melissa: They might die?

Mother: No. You won't know if it's the water or the fertilizer that makes a difference, right? You only want to change one thing, the water. And you only want to look at one result. Not the amount of leaves or how high they grow, but the . . .

Melissa: Number of tomatoes.

Mother: How will the experiment work?

Melissa: I'll have three different tomato plants. And I'll give one quart a day to one, two quarts a day to the second one, and three quarts a day to the third one. After a month I'll count the tomatoes.

Did you notice how the mother guided the child through various stages of the scientific method? I hope you also noticed the development of Melissa's abilities to control variables, keeping them all the same as much as possible—except for the independent variable that she wanted to test. In this case the control variables were light, soil, fertilizer, and time. In many areas of life, work, and relationships, we experiment, controlling for some variables and changing others to see how we can get the best results. You are actually doing this right now by increasing your knowledge (and hopefully practice) for improving conversations with your child.

You will seldom know if a particular conversation and its ideas make a permanent difference, but just consider the power of having many conversations about experimentation over the years.

Analyzing

Analyzing means taking a closer look. It means breaking down a complex event, object, concept, process, or person into its component parts or attributes and then looking at each one in detail. Analyzing also involves recognizing how the parts relate to one another and the roles they play to form the whole thing. It can also involve finding patterns between the components. Other types of analysis involve looking at main claims, errors, feasibility, and validity of arguments.

The ability to analyze depends highly on a person's previous experience and knowledge of how objects, ideas, or concepts can be broken down in the first place. For example, an English teacher's knowledge of literary elements will likely allow her to break down a novel into more dimensions than her friend in the business world. The businessperson, however, will likely find many more ways of breaking down the process of starting and running a successful business than the teacher. The more immersion, challenge, practice—and conversations—a child has in a subject, the better he or she gets at analyzing.

Analyzing is at the core of most school and life tasks. Textbooks, for example, tend to break their subjects down into as many parts as possible in order to provide an in-depth understanding. They often use chapters, headings, and subheadings to describe how they would like readers to analyze and learn a topic. You can help your child improve his or her analysis skills through conversation. Here is an example:

Father: What do you want to know?

Micaela: I heard that some stars don't exist anymore. How can we see them?

Father: That's a great question. Let's take a closer look at light. When you flip on the light switch, what happens?

Micaela: It turns on.

Father: Yes, but actually it turns on and it takes a very little amount of time for the light to travel from the lightbulb to your eyes. You don't notice it at all. Light goes really really fast. If the sun turned off and you had a switch to turn it back on, what might happen?

Micaela: I would have to wait a little bit?

Father: Yeah, around eight minutes. Why?

Micaela: It's really far away.

Father: Yes, now stars are really like suns that are way, way, way much farther away than our sun. And old stars burn out and die sometimes. So if it takes a hundred years for a star's light to reach us, how long will we still look at its light, even after it's dead and gone?

Micaela: A hundred years?

Father: Yes, but why?

Micaela: It's gone, but its light is still going through space.

Notice that the father talked a lot, but he also had some good knowledge to share. And the conversation likely allowed Micaela to stay more engaged and learn more than if it had been a lecture in a classroom. The father also asked a couple of well-placed *why* questions that prompted Micaela to think rather than just rely on him to pour knowledge into her.

Interpreting

Interpreting means watching what happens scientifically (in an experiment or in the real world) and coming up with your own explanation for it. Any time you ask you child, "Why do you think that happened?" you are prompting him or her to interpret. Interpreting can also include deciding if what you see matches your hypothesis or not—and how well it supports it. Interpreting can involve other skills such as measuring, analyzing, comparing, inferring causes and effects, and making conclusions about data.

Here is another conversation between Melissa and her mother about the tomato plants. Look for turns that include some interpreting as well as any prompting for it.

Mother: OK. It's been a month; what did you discover?

Melissa: The two quarts a day won.

Mother: Is that what you predicted?

Melissa: No, I thought it'd be the biggest, the three quarts a day.

Mother: So what do you think happened?

Melissa: I gave a plant one quart a day, one plant two quarts, one three quarts a day. The two-quart plant had the most. It had twenty-seven tomatoes.

Mother: Interesting. How many tomatoes did the others have?

Melissa: The one-quart plant had fifteen, and the three-quart plant had twenty-three.

Mother: So why do you think that happened?

Melissa: I don't know. Maybe the plants don't like too much water, like they drown or something.

Mother: Maybe, or what else might explain it?

Melissa: I don't know. Maybe plants grow different, like people?

Mother: What could you do to be even more certain?

Melissa: I don't know. Maybe try with more plants?

Mother: That might work.

Melissa counted the tomatoes and interpreted the difference between the highly watered plant and the others to conclude that her hypothesis wasn't confirmed. She and her mother then talked about further experimentation to answer the questions and to get more data on more plants (i.e., to increase the sample size of the study).

Point of View Conversations

In this conversation activity, you and your child converse taking the perspectives of a scientific person or thing, such as a scientist, animal, mineral, plant, organism, planet, or object (e.g., river, ocean, mountain, cloud). By being the thing, your child can become more interested and remember it better. Some science things that you and your child can become include a raindrop, moon, glacier, white blood cell, astronaut, galaxy, whale, dinosaur, volcano, spider, guitar, drop of gasoline in a car engine, clam, rock, and star. You can model being something and taking its perspective at first. Then ask your child what he or she wants to be or suggest something. Use a little humor to make it more fun.

Here's an example of a point of view conversation. Notice how the perspective taking is both fun and helpful for strengthening the child's scientific knowledge.

Father: I'm the moon, and you are an astronaut. What do you think you might ask me?

James: What are you made of?

Father: I am made of rock; a lot of it is volcanic. Some come from meteorites that hit me. That's why I have craters. Why are you here, by the way?

James: To learn more.

Father: About what?

James: About the moon, you. Like what you're made of and . . . and like gold, or maybe if any aliens live here.

Father: No, no life lives on me. Do you know why?

James: No water?

Father: Yes, and no air. Not much life can live without air and water.

James: And food.

Father: Unless you can eat rocks. If you could live without all those, you'd be happy here. Lots of great rocks to eat! How did you get here, by the way? I don't get many visitors, you know.

James: In a rocket.

Father: Tell me more.

SUMMARY

The bulk of this chapter focused on using conversations to develop children's science skills of observing, generating good questions, hypothesizing, experimenting, analyzing, and interpreting. These are the most important skills that are needed in science classes and science applications in the real world. As you converse with your child about a wide range of science topics, these skills will help to develop your child's language of science, as well as his or her interest in learning more about how the universe works.

Chapter Six

Conversations about Math

Conversations can build up cities of mathematical ideas in the mind.

Numbers and shapes are all around you, just waiting to be talked about. Daily life offers plenty of math situations and problems that you can talk about with your child. In my research and ongoing work in classrooms, I have noticed a powerful connection between math success and homes where math is discussed. This, of course, makes sense. The more anyone is immersed in ideas about any subject, the more likely they are to acquire a sense of how it works and how to use language to describe it.

So whether you did well in math classes or not, or even whether you like math or not, your conversations with your child about math will have a major impact. This chapter is therefore meant to inspire you to have more and better math-enriching conversations with your child. It describes how conversations can develop mathematical knowledge and skills, and it provides ideas for coming up with topics and further strengthening conversation skills.

BENEFITS OF CONVERSING ABOUT MATH WITH YOUR CHILD

Your Child Learns and Remembers More Math

Conversations can help your child engage in abstract thinking. Math is chock-full of abstractness. A number, let's say 700, represents the quantity of 700 things. There are an infinite number of numbers and an infinite number of things to count. In geometry, a small square on a paper might represent a huge park or the floor of a house. And in algebra, you have a bunch of letters that represent numbers that represent things.

Conversation fosters familiarity (i.e., fluency) with these kinds of abstract ideas. For example, you will usually clarify abstract numerical ideas as you talk with your child. You might also model how to manipulate numbers and symbols, showing how math can be useful for life. Years of exposure to this abstract use of numbers, symbols, and shapes build up, in a good way, to help your child do well in math.

Your Child Builds Mathematical Skills

Conversations offer your child many opportunities to develop mathematical skills. The most important skills are:

- recognizing a mathematical problem or challenge (e.g., buying multiple items at a store, measuring a table, figuring out which area is larger)
- using multiple methods for solving a problem (e.g., using numbers, symbols, diagrams, drawings, actions, gestures, objects, and graphs to show what is happening)
- applying mathematical principles and rules to a situation (e.g., I don't have enough to subtract the lower number, so I borrow a ten from the tens place and add it to the ones place)
- building up mathematical concepts and claims by using problems as examples (division means finding how many times one number fits into another number; for example, six divided by two means two fits into six three times)

Your Child Develops Math Language

Conversations foster your child's abilities to use language that is unique to math. If your child doesn't have some practice in using language to describe math ideas before entering school, he or she might struggle. In conversations, you can model how to say things using math terms and expressions.

For example, when your child wants you to buy four boxes of cookies at the store, you might say, "Wow, what would that cost? If I multiply four times 3 dollars for each box, it's 12 dollars. But two boxes are only two times 3 dollars for each box, which equals 6 dollars. But we can't spend more than 4 dollars on cookies, so how many boxes can we buy?"

Consider the rich language that will grow in your child's mind if he or she talks like this with you multiple times each time you go to the store. As you talk about math over time, your child's brain will borrow and then *own* much of your mathematical language in order to describe his or her own thoughts about math. And then when your child goes to school, he or she will be less stressed and more comfortable talking about math during math lessons.

Your Child Becomes More Interested in Math

Conversations can get your child to be more interested in numbers, shapes, patterns, and solving problems. As your child becomes more "fluent" in talking about math with you, he or she will see the fun challenges that doing math has to offer. For example, when buying a new TV, you talk about comparing the "pay once" option with the monthly payment option. Doing the math, your child sees that the monthly payment option costs a lot more. You talk about why, and your child gets more interested in how monthly payments work.

USING CONVERSATIONS TO BUILD MATHEMATICAL KNOWLEDGE

Math topics do not usually dominate chats with friends, social media exchanges, or casual conversations. Some math might come from playing video games and watching TV shows, but this math is usually not in the forms that students see when they go to school. You, as a parent, need to be intentional, and you might need to brush up on the kind of math your child is learning, especially as your child gets older.

There is a little bit of chicken-egg-ishness here: the more you and your child build up math knowledge, the better your conversations; and the more you converse about math, the more your child's math knowledge develops. So here is a basic "short list" of math topics you can talk about, depending on the age of your child, with some possible questions and prompts for use in conversations.

- Numbers. Your child should understand that each number always means the same quantity of things. The number of toys in the box, let's say three, will be three tomorrow and three a year from now if no toys are taken out or added. Numbers don't get attached to certain items: you can have five cards in one hand and five seeds in the other hand. Sample conversation prompts include:

  - How many candies are in my hand? (Then put your hand behind your back.) Now how many do I have?
  - If we put these coins in a box today and nobody opens it, how many coins will there be tomorrow?
  - I have six rocks in this bag. (Show your hand with six spoons in it.) How many spoons are in my hand?

- One to One. Your child should understand that each thing counted counts as one. You can't count a thing twice. Sample prompts include:

- (Put 6 dimes out.) How many dimes do I have? See if I count them correctly, OK? 1, 2, 3, I like this one so I will count it again, 3, 4, 5. How did I do?
- Why is it hard to count fish in a tank?
- Let's count how many days until your birthday, OK?

- Ordering Quantities. Your child should be able to put quantities in order from smallest to largest and vice versa. It does not depend on their size, color, shape, and so on. Sample prompts include:

  - Can you put toys in a line from toys with no legs, then two legs, then four legs, and so on, with the most-legged toy at the end? Is there another way to arrange them?
  - Let's put the coins into groups and then order them. We can put the smallest number of coins on the left and the largest number on the right. How do you want to start?

- Money. Your child should understand that the two numbers after the decimal stand for cents, which are smaller than a dollar, and there are one hundred of them in one dollar. Sample prompts include:

  - Can you give me change for a dollar? I need 2 quarters, 4 dimes, and 4 nickels, OK?
  - Let's pretend you are buying things from me at the store. If you want to buy this shirt for 20 dollars and this hat for $4.75, how much do you need to pay? Now you sell me some things.
  - If you are at my store and want to buy a toy for $4.75 and you give me 5 dollars, how much change do I owe you?

- Shapes. Your child should understand that shapes with different numbers of sides and curves have names. In some cases, shapes can be split to make other shapes, such as a rectangle cut in half diagonally into two triangles. Sample prompts include:

  - How many circles, squares, rectangles, and squares can we find in this room?
  - Are all squares rectangles? Are all rectangles squares? Why?
  - What can I do to this rectangular piece of paper to make three (or two or four) triangles?

- Length, Perimeter, Weight, Volume, Area. Your child should be able to measure and use measurements of length, weight, volume, and area to solve problems and understand mathematical situations. Use formulas for figuring out perimeters, volumes, and areas. Sample prompts include:

- Is this cord long enough to reach the tree from the house? How can we measure it without walking out to the tree?
- What is the perimeter of the tree trunk? How can we measure it?
- If each board weighs 3 pounds, and we need 40 boards for our tree house, how much will the tree house weigh?
- We need water to drink up there. We have four one-liter bottles of water. How many glasses, which are 200 milliliters each, will we have in total?
- If we make the floor six by five feet, what will be the area of our tree house floor?

- Time. Your child should understand that a year is 365 days, a day is 24 hours, an hour is 60 minutes, and a minute is 60 seconds. Understand that a year has 12 months, which have around 30 days in each. Understand that a week is made up of 7 days. Understand that a half hour is 30 minutes and a quarter of an hour is 15 minutes. Sample prompts include:

  - We are going to Grandma's house in 3 weeks. How many days is that?
  - One year from now, what day will it be? Why?
  - I told you we had to wait for an hour. That was 20 minutes ago. How many minutes do we have left to wait?
  - How many half-hour TV shows can fit into 2 hours of watching?
  - Most commercials are 30 seconds. If they show six commercials, how many minutes out of your life is that?

- Graphs and Tables. Your child should understand and create graphs that show relationships between two sets of numbers on different axes. For example, time is often on the horizontal x-axis and a quantity of things is on the vertical y-axis. Understand and create tables that show relationships between numbers. For example, a table might have holiday names in one column and amount of cards received in the other column that correspond to each holiday. Sample prompts include:

  - How much does your sunflower plant grow each day? How high do you think it will be in 1 month? You can use a graph and predict what it will be. You can put time on the x-axis and what on the y-axis?
  - If you save up 5 dollars per week for that goat (for a family in another country), how many weeks will it take to reach your goal?
  - So on this number table you made more money from your cookie stand on certain days. Why do you think this happened?

- Number Patterns. Your child should be able to recognize patterns in numbers to see how math works. For example, a child notices that every time you add two numbers ending in 5, you get a number ending in 0. Or your child notices that twelve can be divided up into four groups of three, three groups of four, six groups of two, two groups of six. Sample prompts include:

  - What do you notice when you subtract any number from itself?
  - What kinds of groups can you make from these twenty marbles? How many groups of five can you make?
  - What do you notice when you . . . ?

- Addition, Subtraction, Multiplication, Division. Your child should understand how the "big four" operations work. Usually we have two or more numbers that we need to "operate" on in order to produce a different desired number. When you buy things, you add them to get the total cost. When you pay more than the cost, you subtract to know the change. If you buy several of the same item, you multiply; if you want to know the cost per egg in a package of a dozen, you divide the cost by twelve, and so on. Sample prompts include:

  - How are you going to figure out how much money you need in order to buy the ball and the bat?
  - So we ate nine cookies and the box started with twenty-two. How many are left in the box?
  - In each row we planted eight seeds. And there are six rows. How many seeds did we plant?
  - We paid 12 dollars for four bottles of juice, so how much did each one cost?
  - What's the difference between addition and subtraction? Between multiplication and division?

- Fractions and Decimals. Your child should be able to use fractions, decimals, and ratios in real-life situations. Your child should understand how a fraction consists of a numerator, which means the number of parts, over a denominator, which is the "size" of the part of a whole. Two-thirds, for example, means two parts that are each one third the size of a whole thing, whatever it is. A decimal also shows parts of a whole. It tells how many tenths, hundredths, thousandths, and so on, which are to the right of the decimal point, are attached to a whole number, which is on the left of the decimal point. Sample prompts include:

- This pizza has eight pieces. If you eat three-eighths of the pizza, how many pieces do you eat? If I eat one-quarter of the pizza, how many do I eat?
- We just went 8.5 miles and we need to go 10 miles. How many miles do we have left?
- I'll cut you a piece of cake. Would you rather have one-fourth or one-eighth of it? Which one is bigger? Why?
- You are 1.1 meters tall and you need to be 1.5 meters tall to ride the roller coaster. How much do you still need to grow?
- How are fractions and decimals related? What are some examples?

- Variables and Equations. Your child should understand that certain symbols (e.g., variables) can represent various numbers and that you do something with the variables to solve a problem. For example, you could be at the store and ask, "This milk costs 3 dollars a gallon. What if we buy two gallons? What about four gallons? What about ten gallons?" An equation is a mathematical statement of equality that contains one or more variables. To solve an equation, you must figure out which values of the variables work to make the equality true. For example, for the equation $10 - b = 3$, the answer, or solution, is 7 because it makes the equality true. No other number works. An equation is a lot like a balance scale with two sides that weigh the same. If you add or subtract or do anything to one side, you need to do the same to the other. Lots of students change one side and forget to change the other side, which is a mathematical no-no. Sample prompts include:

  - There are three marbles in this blue cup and no marbles in the red cup. If I put four marbles in the red cup, how many do we have? What about if I put two marbles in the red cup? What if I put six or ten or one?
  - This empty box (on paper) stands for an unknown number that makes this equality true. The minus sign means that you take away from that number. This number here is how many we take away. So we have an unknown number minus 2 equals another number, which is a question mark right now. Let's try it. Put a number into the box or tell me a number to put in. (Child says, "8.") OK, 8. Now, say it with me. 8 minus 2 equals . . . what? 6. What about another number for the box?
  - Every time you sweep the patio, you get five new game cards. You already have ten game cards. Let's make an equation that tells us how many game cards you will have, depending on how many times you clean the patio. You get 5 times p, where p is the number of times you clean the patio. We add this to the 10 cards that you already have and you get $5p + 10 = g$, where g is the total number of game cards that you want. Then if you want 50 game cards, we can figure out how many

times you need to clean the patio. We can even draw a graph, if you want to see a drawing of it.

These are just some of the more foundational math concepts and some basic prompts for them. You will think of many more. If your child is in school, you can also take a look at your state's learning standards for mathematics and your child's homework and try to apply some of the math into or from your life. If your child is learning about ratios, for example, and you are watching a show about shark attacks, you can co-create a problem that helps you figure out the size of the shark based on bite marks on a surfboard. The ratio of jaw size to shark length might be 1 to 8 and you converse with your child about different bitemark data and how big the sharks were.

HOW TO USE CONVERSATIONS TO BUILD MATH SKILLS

Here is a list of important mathematical thinking skills synthesized from various sets of K–12 math standards that are often taught in school. Each section describes how conversations can foster these skills.

Recognize and Clarify the Problem

Usually, math conversations involve solving a problem. In many life situations, it is important to recognize what the problem is and what information you need to find. Then it helps to clarify it. The clearer the problem is, the easier it is to solve it. In school, it can be more challenging because children are given a wide range of problems that have nothing to do with their lives. Clarifying a problem means (a) making it clear to yourself and to others what you want to know and (b) organizing the information needed to figure it out.

How Can Conversation Foster This Skill?

In a conversation, you can model clarifying (which is also a general conversation skill), as in the example below, and you can prompt your child to clarify what he or she wants to know. This can include guiding your child to organize information. In fact, one of the main purposes of conversation is for people to use language to clarify ideas for one another. Notice in the following transcript how the father helps the son recognize and clarify the problem and then figure out a way to solve it.

Sam: I lost my cars.

Father: How many cars?

Sam: I don't know.

Father: So you want to know how many cars we are looking for?

Sam: Yeah.

Father: How many do you still have?

Sam: Two.

Father: And you started with how many?

Sam: Five (counts fingers).

Father: So we are looking for how many? You had five in total, right? (shows five fingers on one hand, and then shows just two) And now you have two. How many are lost?

Sam: (counting the closed fingers) Three.

Father: You just did a math problem! You started with five, then subtracted two, and got three. So we are looking for three cars.

Show the Math in Different Ways

In the lost cars transcript, the father used his fingers to represent the numbers in a more concrete way. He was able to make the abstract numbers more concrete. Math is very abstract and uses symbols and other visuals such as graphs, tables, diagrams, and matrices to represent it as clearly as possible.

The more skilled a child is at using representations for math ideas, the better he or she will do in both school math and life math. This includes using multiple representations for the same problem. For example, if a child with a jar of quarters wonders how many quarters she needs to buy a $5.00 candle for her mother, she can (a) draw five circles, divide them into quarter slices, and count the slices; (b) write the fraction ¼ many times and add them up; (c) take out her quarters and stack them in dollar piles until she gets to five; or (d) divide 5.00 by .25 or 500 by 25. Conversations offer opportunities to encourage your child to use different representations, compare them, and give feedback on them.

How Can Conversation Foster This Skill?

In conversations, you can model and suggest different ways to represent the problem. For example, your child is riding a bike in the backyard. You ask, "How many pedal rotations in the same gear would it take you to get to school, without biking all the way to school? You can only go one block away and the school is eight blocks away." You help your child realize that he or she can count the rotations for one block and then add the same number up eight times or, even better, multiply by eight. You can draw this out as you talk about it.

Here is a different conversation excerpt focused on figuring out when a certain number of cookies will be done.

Mother: What are you doing?

Carissa: I want one hundred cookies. I want to know when one hundred cookies'll be done.

Mother: Try drawing it. What do you need to know?

Carissa: One pan, how long is it?

Mother: 10 minutes. But you also need to know how many in a pan, or it's called a batch. Are there one hundred?

Carissa: No. I'll count. Twelve, I think. So, twelve cookies on this pan, batch, with 10 minutes to cook.

Mother: How many pans will we bake?

Carissa: 4 times 12 is . . . 48 cookies; 8 times 12 is 96 cookies, so 9, I guess. Here are nine pans.

Mother: And how about the minutes? That's what you wanted to know.

Carissa: 10 plus 10 plus 10 . . . 90 minutes.

Mother: Great! We can also graph it for fun. Here. For every 12 cookies along the bottom, the line goes up 10 minutes. When I get to 100 cookies, it looks like around 90 minutes, so we're agreed.

Use Multiple Methods for Solving a Problem

In life and math, your child must be good at solving problems in different ways. This means coming up with more than just one approach. Just drawing a problem, for example, might not be accurate enough. You might need to use a "number sentence" with operations in it or a small-scale example to try out ideas. In addition (no pun intended), just one solution method might be a dead end or might contain a mistake. Multiple methods often use different representations. The more practiced your child is at coming up with different methods in a variety of problems, the better. And when your child can compare the methods, even better.

How Can Conversation Foster This Skill?

You can encourage your child to come up with different solution strategies in your conversations. You can use prompts such as:

- Can you think of another way to solve it?
- I think there could be another way to solve it.
- I can think of another way to solve it. Can you?
- How about we try to get the same answer by solving it another way?

Here's a conversation sample that helps to develop this skill.

Elsie: How many pages left?

Father: In the book to read?

Elsie: Yeah.

Father: How can we figure it out?

Elsie: Just tell me.

Father: I can think of two ways to get your answer. Can you?

Elsie: I guess we could just count them up till the end.

Father: That's one way, adding up from where we start, but it takes a while, right? Another way?

Elsie: I don't know.

Father: We know what page we are on, 34, and how many pages in the book, 102, so . . .

Elsie: Add them?

Father: Before trying that, estimate it. About what would you get if you add.

Elsie: Too many, like more than in the book. So, subtract?

Father: Try it.

Elsie: 102 minus 34 . . . it's 68.

Father: Describe how you did that.

Elsie: 2 wasn't enough so I tried to borrow from 0o, but the 0 had nothing, so I borrowed 1 from the 1 and made it a 0, then the 0 into a 10 and borrowed from it; it became a 9; the 2 became a 12, then 12 minus 4 was 8; 9 minus 3 was 6.

Father: Great, and I counted them like you said and got 68, too. Now, how are these methods connected?

Elsie: In subtract, I took away 34 from 102. In counting, you started at 34 to get to 102; you kinda took it away 'cause you started there at 34.

Notice how the father encourages Elsie to think of two methods and then compare them at the end. He also has her describe her thinking for the subtraction process to get her to practice verbalizing math language and processes.

Make Logical Statements (Claims and Arguments) and Support Them by Using Mathematical Rules and Principles

Children do not always use typical reasoning to solve problems, so it helps to use conversations to immerse them in using more adult-like mathematical reasoning. In math lessons in school (and in life), your child will need to make claims and support them mathematically.

For example, a child might notice that with 12 pennies she can make three groups of four or two groups of six or four groups of three. She says, "I can make different groups. But I can't make five groups that are the same. I can make six groups of two. I can't split twelve up for five. See? I get two groups of five and a group of two." Notice this child's foundational understandings of multiplication and division here.

How Can Conversation Foster This Skill?

In conversations, you can prompt your child to come up with interesting mathematical ideas and also support them with mathematical reasoning. You can ask questions such as:

- What can you do to find the answer? Why?
- If you do that, what will happen to the number?
- What math rule can you come up with?
- Do you think that is always true? Sometimes true? Never true?
- What problems help to show your idea about how math works?

Here's a conversation sample that includes supporting an idea for how to solve a problem.

Mother: We just bought five malt balls for 50 cents. I wonder how much one malt ball would cost.

Alex: 5 cents?

Mother: How did you get that?

Alex: I don't know. A dollar?

Mother: Wait. Would just one cost more than five cost?

Alex: No.

Mother: It would cost less than 50 cents. What can we do with 50 cents?

Alex: Buy more?

Mother: Funny. No. We can split it up.

Alex: Like this. Five groups. Five malt balls.

Mother: So each one would cost, what?

Alex: 10 cents.

Mother: So what do we do when we have a problem like this one again? It won't always be 10 cents.

Alex: We make groups. Split it up into same groups?

Notice and Use Mathematical Patterns

An essential skill in mathematics is noticing and using geometrical or numerical patterns. Geometrical patterns include any types of repeating lines such as lines in the sidewalk, shapes such as triangular windows on a building, or three-dimensional objects such as boxes stacked in the garage.

Numerical patterns tend to be more abstract, including noticing that you can count a quantity of things in any order and get the same number; the denominator of a fraction is the number of fraction pieces that make one whole; adding a zero to the end of a number multiplies it by ten; the area of rectangle is always base times height, and so forth. As your child gets older, he or she will need to notice more and more the patterns that show how math works.

In school, your child will do many math problems. These problems are meant to teach mathematical concepts. Resist the temptation that many schools have fallen into, which is teaching shortcuts for getting problems right (usually to improve test scores) quickly. Shortcuts shortchange your child's understandings and mathematical reasoning.

When you create and solve math problems with your child, talk about how math is full of patterns and ideas. When your child says, "You gotta divide because that's what we're working on this week," respond with, "OK, but in life you need to choose different ways to solve problems and have good reasons for them. You need to see patterns and know how math works. So what is division and why do it in this problem or other problems?"

How Can Conversation Foster This Skill?

Through conversation, you can help your child notice a variety of math-related patterns in the world. Here are some prompts that might help:

- So do you think we can find any patterns out here in nature, like looking at plants or trees or waves on the water or the rocks?
- I bet we can find three different patterns on that building over there. What do you think?
- What do we do when we see problems like this one, when we need to find a fraction of another fraction? Why?
- If we want to know the total price of these four things, what do we do? What do we always do at the store to find the final cost?
- What patterns do you see in that painting (photograph, sculpture)? What math could we do with it?

Here is sample conversation in which the mother prompts Leigh to look for mathematical patterns in what they are observing on a walk. The insight in the last line is especially interesting.

Mother: How many trees do you think are in that orchard right there?

Leigh: I don't know.

Mother: What do you notice? Any patterns that might help?

Leigh: They're in rows. Like I look this way and that way and that way, and I can see rows each way.

Mother: Hmmm. What does that mean?

Leigh: I don't know. It's like a design, maybe. Maybe there are rows this way and if you go around the corner you might see like this side here.

Mother: So how can we figure out how many there are without counting them all? Here's a smaller version (draws four rows of four circles). How many circles are there?

Leigh: Sixteen.

Mother: Yes, you counted them, right?

Leigh: Yeah.

Mother: Look. It's also 4 plus 4 plus 4 plus 4. 4 times 4, right?

Leigh: Yeah.

Mother: Now if I put two more rows of four on, it's 6 times 4, right?

Leigh: Yeah.

Mother: So? . . . How might that help us with the trees?

Leigh: Maybe count one side and then the other?

Mother: And then?

Leigh: Then multiply them. It's like area, but it's not the area. It's trees.

Get into the Hobby of Math-Watching

Like birdwatching, it helps to build up your abilities to look out for math in all corners of the day. Look for mathematical things, like many of the examples you just saw above, that can become conversation topics and problems. Get into the habit of looking around for numbers and other math concepts such as shapes, patterns, probabilities, costs, and so on and wondering something about them.

At a shopping center, for example, you might wonder how many bricks are in the patio, how many leaves are on a tree, how long it will take the beam of sunlight to move across the patio, how many gallons of paint it will take to paint a storefront wall, the percentage of flower seeds that will bloom in the planter boxes. Modeling this type of thinking will help you and your child to have conversations about a wide range of mathematical topics that are right in front of you.

You ultimately want your child to do a lot of math-watching and wondering. The more your child develops this habit, the more engaged in the conversation he or she will be. At first, you model the wondering in various situations, and you will also guide the conversations that you have about the math. You might look at a box of cereal and say, "I wonder how many servings I would need to cover 100 percent of my daily recommended allowance for Vitamin A. How can we figure this out?" Or "We just drove 500 miles on a 15-gallon tank of gasoline. I wonder how many miles per gallon that is."

Other number wonderings include:

- I wonder how long it will take that jet to reach New York if it's going 600 miles per hour.
- I wonder how many showers' worth of water are in that pool.
- I wonder what fraction of that glass of milk you just drank.
- I wonder what the probability is of rolling a two on those dice.
- I wonder how much that toy will cost with sales tax?
- I wonder how many square feet of carpet we would need to cover this room.
- I wonder how many spoons we have in the drawer.
- I wonder how many leaves are on that tree.
- I wonder how many bricks are in that wall.
- I wonder when we'll get to St. Louis.
- I wonder how many points she averages per game.
- I wonder how much sugar to put in if we triple the recipe.
- I wonder how many different ways a football team can score thirty-eight points.
- I wonder how much 5 gallons of milk would cost.
- I wonder how many square feet of carpet there are in that room.

After plenty of wonder modeling, you can ask, "What numbers (or shapes) do you wonder about?" to prompt your child to come up with possible conversation topics. When he or she responds, you can then start a conversation about the idea or the problem. And remember that a good conversation will tend to include conversation skills such as listening, clarifying, supporting, and so on.

Here is a sample conversation that took place at the store. Notice the conversation moves used by the mother to prompt the child to think and use math skills in an engaging way.

Mother: Look at all the cereal in this aisle. Do you have any math questions?

Samuel: How many boxes are there?

Mother: Hmmm. I don't know. How would you estimate the number?

Samuel: I don't know. Count them?

Mother: Sure, but that wouldn't be an estimate, and it would take a lot of time. We estimate when we don't have much time.

Samuel: OK. One hundred.

Mother: How did you estimate that?

Samuel: I just guessed.

Mother: An estimate is a good guess. You should have a reason for it and use some math. Start with a sample, say, with one type of cereal.

Samuel: This one, Cap'n Crunch. Can we get a box?

Mother: No. Too much sugar. Now count them.

Samuel: You said not to count them.

Mother: I said not to count all of them on the aisle. It doesn't take long to count just one type.

Samuel: OK. Eight boxes.

Mother: Now what?

Samuel: So. Eight boxes of this cereal. So I count the different cereals?

Mother: Yes, the types of each one. Try it.

Samuel: Twenty.

Mother: OK. Then what?

Samuel: Times it by eight?

Mother: Try it.

Samuel: One hundred sixty, right?

Mother: That sounds like a good estimate to me.

SUMMARY

Math is usually not the first thing that comes to mind when asked what to converse about. Yet talking with your child about math can make huge differences in his or her mathematical knowledge and practices in school and life. Many children need to use and talk about math outside of school in order to learn it in depth. Try some of the ideas in this chapter, and you will likely see the differences that conversations about math can make for your child.

Chapter Seven

Conversations That Grow the Heart

A solo blade of grass withers in the wind.

The previous chapters focused on using conversations to grow your child's mind. Now it's time to look at ways to nurture your child's heart through conversation. The heart is the central hub for your child's feelings, values, and personality traits. Just like the roots under trees, a person's feelings, values, and traits are deep and difficult to change. That's why you must get started early and keep going for, well, a long time.

Conversation, fortunately, is a powerful way to positively shape a child's heart over time. It often takes many conversations to do this shaping, but it is what you signed up to do when you became a parent. It is also one of the most exciting parts of raising a child; that is, to be supportive as your child blossoms into a wonderful person.

In a nutshell, you want to increase positive and constructive feelings, values, and traits, and you want to decrease the negative and destructive ones. Figure 7.1 includes some sample lists of things in each column.

As you can see in the chart, there is a lot going on in the heart. This is just a sample that I am trying to use with my children. As I made these lists, I realized that most of these are things that I am still trying to increase and decrease in my own life. And as I converse with my children, I share with them how I am trying to change over time. This is one way in which they see that growing to be better people is a lifelong process.

CONVERSING TO CULTIVATE FEELINGS

As you already know, influencing a child's feelings through conversation or any other means is messy business. Some say that we shouldn't even try. But

♡	*Increase*	*Decrease*
Feelings	Confidence, empathy, happiness, gratitude, hope	Selfishness, inferiority, anger greed, hatred, fear, arrogance
Values	kindness, sharing, honesty, justice, family, love, communication,	things over people, just getting by, winning at all costs,
Traits	caring, patient, creative, curious, trustworthy, ethical, respectful, generous, patient, humble	unethical, impatient, disrespectful, dishonest, lazy, arrogant

Figure 7.1.   Sample Lists of Feelings, Values, and Traits to Increase and Decrease

your child's feelings are already influenced by a wide range of things, including conversations that they have with you and with others. It is helpful, even vital, to consider how to nurture the feelings that you think should be nurtured. I include several examples in this section of feelings that I am trying to foster in my children through conversations with them.

As I have mentioned often in this book, there are no guarantees—especially when dealing with the heart. If growth does happen, it is slow. Be patient and diligent, and keep trying and talking.

Converse to Cultivate Happiness

One of the main reasons you are reading this book is because you want your child to be happy. Definitions of happiness vary a lot, of course, but most of them involve having positive feelings about something, such as being at a party, receiving a gift, doing well on an exam, winning a game, and so on. Yet even more important is cultivating your child's ongoing feelings of happiness in response to more common things in life, such as spending time with family, playing with friends, being outdoors, seeing new things, meeting new people, reading, and simply being alive.

Here is a sample conversation focused on happiness.

Mother: Are you happy at school?

Ben: Not really.

Mother: Why not?

Ben: I don't know.

Mother: Did anything happen?

Ben: Devin's team won the math contest, and I wanted our team to win it.

Mother: That's disappointing. I would feel that way, too. But did you try your hardest?

Ben: Yes.

Mother: And did you have fun with your team during the contest?

Ben: Up until we lost.

Mother: So you tried your hardest, you learned a lot, and you had fun with your team. You can be happy about those things, right?

Ben: I guess.

Mother: And you can be happy for Devin's team, right?

Ben: What?

Mother: One important lesson I learned when I was a bit older than you is to be happy when others win. I still try my hardest, but if, in the end, they win and are happy, I am happy, too. Sometimes, if they are sad about losing, I actually wish I had lost. Isn't that weird?

Ben: You mean like when I let Sara (sister) score goals on me?

Mother: Yes. One of the best ways to be happy is to help make others happy and to be happy for others when they're happy.

Notice how Ben's mother uses the conversation as a chance to help him reflect on how to be happy in ways other than winning. The conversation nurtures a bit of empathy as well.

Converse to Cultivate Emotional Awareness and Empathy

Emotional awareness means being able to recognize how other people are feeling and understand why they might feel that way. This awareness helps a child care for others and better understand him- or herself. These days, many challenges exist that tend to inhibit growth in this area. There are many non-face-to-face modes of communication (e.g., social media), video games, TV and movies, and so on. As children spend more time with these, they tend to spend less time understanding the feelings of real people. Conversations can help to grow a child's abilities and interest in how others feel.

Conversations can help a child develop emotional awareness by talking about three things: (a) what has happened or is happening to influence a person's feelings; (b) facial expressions and body language; and (c) what the person says and how he or she says it.

Here's a sample conversation. Notice how the father fostered empathy skills.

Father: Do you know why your mother is sad?

Belén: She's tired?

Father: No, she wanted to read to you to put you to sleep, but you just wanted to play with your toys.

Belén: I like to play with the toys.

Father: Yes, but we all need to see how others feel. Your mom just wanted to spend time with you. Did you see her face? In our family, we love each other and so we try to make each other happy. How would you feel if she said that she would rather play video games than read to you, if you asked her to read to you?

Belén: Sad.

Father: Why?

Belén: Because I want Mommy to read with me.

Father: And you probably want her to show you she loves to spend time with you. She gets sad when she thinks you don't want to be with her.

Belén: Yeah. Sorry.

Notice how the father encouraged Belén to think about her mother's feelings and put herself into her mother's shoes. It is difficult for many younger children to empathize as well as adults, but conversations like this one can help. Conversations can teach children how others tend to feel in certain situations.

Converse to Understand Love

Life is full of abstract and powerful things, and one of the most important is love. Love is quite deep and broad, so I only provide a taste of how you might talk about it in this brief section. First off, love is an emotional and active commitment to the well-being of another person. To love someone means wanting the best for that person and acting to help him or her have a great life. Love is often two-way: you want the best for the other person, of course, but you also want to be with the other person because this will help you to have a great life.

When you talk about love with your child, you can emphasize several components of love: patience, kindness, self-sacrifice, forgiveness, commitment, desire, and so forth. In fact, many of these components are values, which are discussed more in depth later in this chapter.

Here is a brief conversation between a mother and her daughter about love.

Mother: When I say "I love you," do you know what that means?

Nyla: You really like me?

Mother: Yes, but way more. I want to spend time with you; I want the very best for you. I would give my life for you.

Nyla: I love you, too.

Mother: Why?

Nyla: Because you're my mom.

Mother: Any other reasons? I ask because sometimes people you love like to hear why.

Nyla: You are really nice. You do lots of things for me. You make me laugh. You hug and kiss me. Sometimes I don't like that, but sometimes I do. Why do you love me?

Mother: Because you are so kind to me and others. And you are full of life and joy. And you give me hugs, too, when I need them. And a thousand other reasons.

Notice how Nyla's mother helps her to see the various reasons for loving others as well as the various ways to love others. Consider the power of having many conversations like this one over the years.

LOVING YOUR CHILD THROUGH CONVERSATION

While much of this chapter is on what to talk about with your child, including love, this box emphasizes how you can love *through* conversation. First, you can show love by talking to your child. Some parents are busy doing too many things to have good conversations with their children. Second, talk about topics that interest your child. Don't just bring up topics that interest you or that make your child feel like he or she is being lectured. Third, you can tell your child you love her at appropriate spots in the conversation, even saying something like, "I love you so much and I love talking with you about . . . " Fourth, you can focus and listen well during the conversation. You can be silent, and you can prompt your child to talk about his or her feelings, thoughts, dreams, plans, ideas, inventions, projects, questions, and so forth. Fifth, you can show love through posture, gestures, eye contact, smiling, and physical contact. These sound obvious, but with so many screen-based distractions throughout the home these days, such communication can be rare.

CONVERSING TO CULTIVATE VALUES

Values are the things that matter to people, and they tend to range from concrete to abstract. Concrete values include things such as money, houses, vacations, cars, clothes, hobbies, sports, people, video games, entertainment, and so on. Abstract values include solitude, peace, freedom, rights, knowledge, status, communication, reason, honesty, nature, excellence, integrity, justice, service, organization, teamwork, and citizenship. We all have a muddy mix of these values, and they tend to play both leading and supporting roles in how we live each day.

We can't value everything equally, so we "choose" certain values to put at the top of our invisible (and changing) lists for how we think about and how we "do" life. Different people value different things—and, sometimes, different things on different days. This makes life much more interesting. You might value planning ahead more than spontaneity, and your spouse might value freedom more than comfort. You might value friendship more than winning, and your friend might value honesty more than money.

What we value often shapes our heart, the essence of who we are. In other words, what we think about, what our minds tend to drift toward and focus on, is what we value. And what we think about often depends on what we spend time doing (e.g., playing video games, watching TV, reading the news, reading books, playing sports, painting pictures). So, in order to nurture positive values in your child, you need to (a) be a good model and make sure that you are valuing the things that help your heart to grow and (b) have conversations with your child about the idea that what he or she values will shape his or her heart over time.

Your values often play large roles in how you live life and relate to others. Yet they are also somewhat fluid, difficult to nail down, and hard to define on any given day. For this reason, you and your child can use conversations to clarify and negotiate what you value, why, and how much. And your child needs to be able to talk about his or her own values as well as those of others.

Yet even before talking about values with your child, it helps to clarify what *you* value, why you value it, and how you decide what to value in life. Think about what you choose to do in your "free" time. Do you read, play games, exercise, watch TV, paint, play with your child, cook, do extra work for your job, shop, spend time online, and so on? Think about what you tend to think about. The more common topics are sports, religion, work, family, possessions, home improvement, traveling, the future, the past, finances, and friends. Which ones get more mental limelight?

You also have a set of more abstract values, such as honesty, peace, courage, perseverance, communication, humor, wisdom, tradition, reputation, spontaneity, empathy, success, simplicity, discipline, self-control, planning ahead, happiness, creativity, relaxation, reason, practicality, commitment, diligence, justice, kindness, loyalty, love, independence, harmony, gratitude, growth, and so forth. You might also have some not-so-good values such as power, control, winning at all costs, beauty, revenge, status, and the like. Make a list with your top values at the top. Then consider which of these you want your child to have and not have.

Once you have a clearer idea of what you value and why, you are more ready to talk about values with your child. Below are a few tips for using conversations to define and build up values in your child.

Converse about the Values That Influence *Your* Actions and Words

You can talk about your own actions and words and the values that drive them. You might talk about why you work, why you donate money to charity, why you like to go camping, why you like to read certain types of novels, or why you use social media. What you do tends to stem from values that you have for how you use your time. If you like to travel, for example, you might value learning new languages, eating exotic foods, or just getting away from the bustle of your current routines.

In the following conversation, the mother talks about one of her hobbies, cooking. Notice the values that come out in the conversation.

Timo: Why don't you just cook easy things?

Mother: Good question. It would be easier and maybe cheaper. But I like the creativity of it. It's like art.

Timo: What?

Mother: Well, I take new ingredients and put them together and something new comes out that we can eat.

Timo: But it takes longer, and sometimes it's weird.

Mother: Sorry about the weird stuff, but it also takes my mind off of work; all I have to think about is measuring and mixing and tasting something new. Do you have anything like cooking, where you create or build new things?

Timo: I like to do Legos.

Mother: What do you like about putting them together?

Timo: I like that I can make anything I want and I don't know what it is until I finish it. Sometimes I even decide what it is after I look at it.

Mother: So you value being creative and building things. My cooking is like that.

Converse about the Values That Influence Your Child's Actions and Words

As you saw at the end of the previous conversation, you can talk about the values that influence what your child does and says. You can start by noticing what your child spends time doing and talking about. Ask why he or she likes to do things such as playing video games, playing with trains, going on hikes, playing a sport, reading certain books, drawing, and so on. Values will often emerge. When a positive value comes up, you can name it, encourage your child to continue having it, and describe how it can be useful in other areas of life.

Here's a sample conversation.

Father: So, Edgar, why do you really like to play soccer?

Edgar: I guess I like running around and being with my friends.

Father: Why do you like to be around friends?

Edgar: I don't know. I like to be on a team; you know, we have fun and laugh and stuff.

Father: What about when you lose?

Edgar: I don't like to lose, but some teams are better than us. And I still get to run around.

Father: I like your values. You value friends and exercise more than winning.

Edgar: Well, I like to win and want to win, but I see some kids that it's like the end of the world if they lose. It's a bit messed up.

Father: Yeah, some people get so focused on winning that they don't enjoy life much, even when they do win. I actually valued winning too much at your age, and then I realized that friends were much more important. So keep on valuing your friendships and being a good friend, win or lose.

Edgar: OK.

In some cases, you might want to "reduce" certain unproductive values. A child might say that he likes to play video games because he doesn't want to play with other children. This is an opportunity to talk about the importance of learning how to play with others, how to win and lose respectfully, how to be creative alongside others, how to value others, and so on.

Another child might say that she wants to look prettier than all the other girls, in which case the parent can sit down with her and converse about the value of one's personality and heart ("it's the inside that counts") and how society pressures people to look like movie stars and magazine models. Additional values that you might want to "reduce" include focusing on winning, cheating, showing off, spending too much time online, giving in to peer pressure, wanting to watch violent shows, and so forth.

Consider the following conversation in which Arturo's mother tries to instill in Arturo the value of practicing.

Arturo: I hate school.

Mother: Why?

Arturo: I have to do homework. But there is a lot of it, and I don't have time to play video games 'cause you make me do it.

Mother: Why do you think they have you do homework?

Arturo: 'Cause for grades, you know, points.

Mother: What about your learning? You practice things in homework, right?

Arturo: I guess. But it's boring. I don't think I learn much from it.

Mother: And when you play video games, do you get better at them?

Arturo: Yes, 'cause video games are fun.

Mother: But not all things in life are fun, right? And even if you don't learn a lot from homework, it is part of being a student, and it helps you practice skills that you learn. I need to practice computer skills for my job. So what does that mean for your homework?

Arturo: Practice helps me learn and be a student, I guess.

Mother: You value practice in video games and just need to spread that value over into schoolwork.

Arturo: I'll try.

This one conversation might not have permanently established the value of practice in Arturo. But many conversations like this one over time will likely help this value grow. Even if Arturo never openly admits or realizes that he is valuing practice more over time, his behaviors and choices will hopefully show this value.

Converse about What Others Value and Do Not Value

On most days, your child observes other people who do and say things that show their values. It might be another student at school who offers to help your child do something. It might be a person on TV who risks her life to save a friend. It might be a grandparent who spends time with a grandchild.

Notice that I chose to focus on positive values here. It is easy to see negative things that people do and talk badly about them. Many people, unfortunately, develop the habit of criticizing others and gossiping. While they may be right about another person's lack of values in some area, talking about it too much isn't a good habit (or value) to develop. Therefore, try to model and help your child see the good in people, to notice the good things that they do and say, and to assume positive values.

Here's a sample conversation. Notice how Julia's mother gets her to think about how much she values a friendship with someone who makes fun of others.

Julia: I saw my friend make fun of a new student in our class. Other students laughed.

Mother: Did you?

Julia: No. I felt bad. But I thought I should laugh.

Mother: Why?

Julia: 'Cause she's my friend.

Mother: You did right. Even though it's really hard to go against a friend and maybe even lose her, you valued the new student's feelings. I'm proud of you.

Julia: But I don't have a lot of friends.

Mother: You don't have to lose her as a friend, but you can talk to her.

Julia: And say what?

Mother: You can say that you didn't think it was funny to make the new student feel bad.

Julia: What if she doesn't want to be my friend?

Mother: Do you want someone who doesn't want to change to be your friend?

Julia: No.

Because we can't value everything equally (if we did, they wouldn't be values), we need to compare values to choose the ones that we think are most important. Conversations that compare and argue the importance of values can be very fruitful. For example, if your child is choosing between watching TV and finishing homework, you can talk about the value of entertainment versus the value of learning and completing tasks. You can't precisely measure the weight of the values to make a decision, but the conversations can help your child understand that he or she is usually comparing values when choosing what to do in life.

Get to know your child's values. Use the list of positive and negative values included in figure 7.1 as a guide. Reflect on how often your child shows evidence of a value and the result of having it. Then choose several values that you think (a) are very important to have (or not have) and (b) that your child seems to need to improve.

Converse about Priorities for What Enters the Heart

Memories play a large role in who we are and what we value. For example, I might remember an incident in which my mother helped my father when he was sick. This memory sticks with me and reminds me of the values of selfless love and true commitment in a marriage. Then again, I might also remember a time when I was bullied or cheated and still have thoughts that dwell on (or, in other words, "value") vengeance, rather than valuing forgiveness and moving on in life. We can use conversations to help children retain helpful memories and try to diminish the more negative ones.

Each mind only has so much room. If you fill it up with some things, you don't have room for others. There is a lot of information and ideas available these days. And a lot of "sellers" of products and ideas are trying to get into your child's head. Be a model for what you choose to take in, and talk to your child about what he or she chooses. Help him or her to make the most "mentally and heart-fully healthy choices," just as if they were choosing what food to put into their bodies.

Through conversation, you can help your child make better choices from a young age. He or she can choose to: write positive things when using social media, play educational games and limit time playing them, not watch violent or scary shows, not focus on other people's flaws or mistakes, and respect and appreciate how others are different.

Here is a sample conversation.

Shari: I don't know why I watch that show.

Father: Why do you say that?

Shari: It's about kids my age, so I thought it was good. But they lie and play tricks on each other.

Father: So why do you watch it?

Shari: They . . . like my friends watch it, so they talk about it and I want to know what's going on, you know.

Father: Yes, but is it worth it?

Shari: How?

Father: Well, you end up thinking about what you watch, like it fills your head up with whatever you watch.

Shari: Yeah, but I like talking about it with my friends.

Father: Maybe you can find some other shows to talk about.

Shari: Maybe, but I think they like the bad stuff they watch.

Father: Yeah. So maybe you just say something like, "I don't watch that show anymore."

Shari: I guess.

Father: It sounds like that show doesn't make you happy, and it isn't good for your heart, so choosing to watch other shows in your limited TV time is a good choice.

CONVERSING TO CULTIVATE CHARACTER TRAITS

Character traits are the qualities of your child's personality that make him or her different from others. Here I include a "short list" of traits that you might want to develop in your child through conversation: positive, enthusiastic, ethical, a good listener, persistent, flexible, patient, kind, compassionate, brave, diligent, forgiving, creative, curious, unselfish, lighthearted, grateful, honest, humble, friendly, joyful, committed, loyal, down to earth, sincere, trustworthy, good communicator, respectful, flexible, and so on. There are about as many negative traits, too, many of which you can come up with by putting "not" or "un-" in front of the positive ones.

Remember, genes do play a role in a person's character traits but not 100 percent. Your conversations and your modeling of traits can and do shape your child's traits over time. This is as much true for positive traits as it is for negative ones. So we must be extra aware of our own traits, especially the negative ones, because we tend to not see our negatives as well as our positives.

This section focuses on how you can have conversations that develop positive traits and reduce negative traits in your child over time. I have chosen several traits as examples of how to develop them in conversation, but feel free to develop your own list of the traits that you want your child to develop.

Grateful

We frequently tell children to say "Thank you," but too often we get the sense that they are just being polite and will say it just to make us happy. What we want is for our children to have a true feeling of gratitude for the many people, experiences, and things that they have. Why is gratitude so important? It keeps children (and adults) from a sense of entitlement, the feeling that they deserve all of the good things that come their way. And with respect to people, they like you better if you are thankful for them, the time they spend with you, and the things they do for you. Relationships go bad when one or both don't appreciate the other.

Is your child grateful for his or her bed, electricity, the heater in winter, food in the fridge, you, your spouse, siblings, clothes, being able to see, friends, school, health, and so on? Many kids aren't. They have come to think that they deserve, despite very little effort on their part, a mountain of things and services in life. Without gratitude, even for basic things, your child can easily become entitled, spoiled, and even—perish the thought—whiny.

Being grateful helps a child to be content in the present, without that gnawing stress of needing more things to be happy. It also fosters humility because the child is not constantly thinking, "I deserve . . . " This attitude can, in part, stem from being immersed in a sea of advertisements that tell kids to want more and that they can't be happy without such things. Talk about this phenomenon. Talk about how companies invest billions of dollars to hook kids into wanting things that they don't need.

One way to foster gratitude in your conversations is to model your own gratitude for the many things, people, and experiences you enjoy in life. For example, on a walk, you are thankful for the beautiful view, trees that provide shade, the ability to walk and see and smell, and so on.

Here is a conversation sample in which the mother helps her daughter to be more thankful for people and common things in life.

Mother: What are you thankful for?

Daniela: Presents. But I don't have any.

Mother: I mean what things every day that you have. Like I am thankful for you and for the food we get to eat every day and for our heater.

Daniela: OK, for me I like toys.

Mother: Which toys are you thankful for?

Daniela: The little piano, horsey, Thomas the Train.

Mother: Anything else?

Daniela: I like ice cream and cookies.

Mother: Yes, me too. But are you thankful for your bed? Our house? The rain? Me?

Daniela: Yes. And Edie, too, and Daddy. And Grandma. And socks.

Mother: Socks? Why?

Daniela: I don't like my feet cold.

Mother: I agree!

Caring, Kind, Friendly, Empathetic, Unselfish

These overlapping traits tend to depend on a person's ability to suspend his or her own desires to understand and act on what other people need and want. Persons with these traits do and say things that make others feel liked and important. These traits are vital for living and working with others in the world. Just consider a world where the opposite traits dominate: where people are mean, unfriendly, antisocial, lone rangers, inconsiderate of others' feelings, and selfish. This isn't how humans grow and thrive. We are meant to meet one another's needs, to work together, to listen, and to grow in relationships with others that benefit them first and us second. You want your child to not only live in such a world but to contribute to its growth.

One of the most important traits that children (and everyone else) should have is caring about and for others. This sounds obvious, but as we all know, children (and adults) tend to devote a lot of mental energy to caring about themselves. The obsession with one's own desires and needs ranges from very high to moderate, but we all zoom up and down the spectrum on a daily basis. So how can conversations get children to care about others? Here are some ideas (though not final answers) for addressing this question. You can try them out and see what happens.

A large part of caring is understanding how the person thinks and feels, also called empathy. But children don't always tend toward empathy. Conversations can actually build students' capacities to think about how other people think and feel. For example, in this conversation, the mother prompts the child to consider how the boy in the story felt about losing his pet cat.

Mother: What happened?

Josh: Boy lost a cat.

Mother: How did the boy feel?

Josh: Bad.

Mother: What do you mean when you say bad?

Josh: He liked it. He lost it. He liked its meow. He was a friend.

Mother: I agree. I think he felt sad, too. But how do you think the boy will feel if the cat comes back?

Josh: Good.

Mother: Because?

Josh: 'Cause he'll get his friend back.

Mother: I agree. I think he will feel ecstatic to hug his friend and hear him purr again.

As you can see in this conversation, the mother prompts her son to think about the feelings of another, in this case a character in a story. But you can also ask your child how others might feel in a wide range of situations, such as after having an argument with a schoolmate, watching a TV show, walking past a homeless person, playing with other children, sharing toys, and so forth. Of course, like most of the skills in this book, you need a lot of conversations about a range of topics over time. Conversations about the feelings of others won't do much if they happen infrequently. Building the heart takes loads of time and practice.

In addition to considering the feelings of others, caring also involves thinking about what others need or want in order to make them happy. How wonderful it is when your child responds to your needs or predicts what you might need or want—and then does something about it. Conversations, not surprisingly, can help to build children's mental pathways and habits for thinking about others' needs.

For example, in the following conversation, the father prompts his daughter to predict the needs of her mother.

Father: Alicia, you know what Mommy likes?

Alicia: No.

Father: Surprises.

Alicia: I do, too. Like the party for my birthday where everyone jumped and . . .

Father: Alicia, what kind of surprise do you think your mother would like?

Alicia: Chocolate?

Father: Yes, that's always nice, but what can you do for her that would really surprise her and make her extra happy? What does she like?

Alicia: She likes things clean. I could clean my room.

Father: You need to clean your room anyway. How about something that you don't already need to do?

Alicia: I could dust the living room.

Father: Nice idea. How do you think you might feel when you see her smile?

Alicia: Good.

Ethical

Being ethical means living by a code of sound moral principles. It means choosing what is right over what is wrong. In most people, there is an innate sense of right and wrong regarding most topics. It's wrong to lie, steal, hurt, cheat, break the law, and so on. Other topics take a bit more thought, such as buying certain products made by mistreated factory workers, driving a car that pollutes the air, watching violent movies, paying for an expensive hobby, and so forth. It helps your child to talk about the variety of ethical dilemmas that people face in life.

Notice in the following conversation how the mother helps Mei to think about the ethics of a situation.

Mei: Look at this flower!

Mother: It's beautiful, Mei, but we really shouldn't pick flowers in the park.

Mei: Why not?

Mother: Can you think of a reason?

Mei: Maybe there's a rule about it?

Mother: Maybe, but even if there's no rule, could there be a reason?

Mei: 'Cause it dies?

Mother: Yes, that's a good reason, but also remember that lots of people visit the park. What will happen if everyone picks them?

Mei: None left.

Mother: So?

Mei: We shouldn't pick flowers because so everyone can see them.

Mother: Yes, we need to share public things, like things in parks and out in nature.

Confident and Self-Assured

Confidence is belief in one's self. It means feeling assured in one's abilities to do or be something and believing in one's own abilities to get things done and learn what needs to be learned. It means feeling and believing that with hard work, patience, and practice, one can get better at something and succeed.

We want our children to be confident that they can overcome challenges and make significant changes in the world. We want them to (a) believe that they can improve in whatever they want or need to do and (b) not believe that they don't have abilities to do it.

Conversations can play a large role in feelings of self-confidence. Here is a sample focused on building a child's artistic confidence.

Mother: I like how you kept on trying to paint those mountains.

Abigail: I'm not an artist.

Mother: You are an artist. Artists paint things many times. And it takes them years to get really good.

Abigail: I don't want to wait years.

Mother: You're already doing great! Look at how you mixed the colors on that mountain! It's gorgeous!

Abigail: I kinda like that one, too. Not sure how, or like if I can do it again.

Mother: Try it again and again. Have fun. Maybe after a while you can put on an exhibit and show your paintings to the family.

Abigail: No way.

Self-confidence, self-esteem, and self-assuredness are related terms. We should want all children, for example, to have enough self-confidence to not shy away from challenges and to press on over time in order to improve or learn or accomplish something. They should believe that they are capable of learning, growing, improving.

Yet some children have the idea that they were born with or without certain abilities. They have a rigid view of these abilities, which can include social, physical, linguistic, and intellectual skills. The important thing is to keep discussing this misconception so that they can improve in all skills. They might never play in the NBA or in Carnegie Hall, but they can improve in all things and become very good at most things if they view that growth as possible and if they work hard. Conversations can play a large role in shaping this view, as you can see in the following sample.

Father: How do you like your math class?

David: I'm no good at math.

Father: Why do you say that?

David: 'Cause I can't solve all the problems.

Father: I've seen you get better at everything you have tried. You will get better at math.

David: Not if I don't like it.

Father: Lots of things in life you won't like. When new things come up in my job, I don't like them all. But I push myself to believe I can do them. You can learn anything. It just takes work and practice.

David: OK.

Persistent and Patient

Being persistent means being able to keep going in the face of adversity and setbacks, being patient in the pursuit of goals, and not giving up despite big challenges. It means putting in hard work over long periods of time. Persistence is vital in life because we seldom have easy paths laid out before us. Persistence tends to require being patient and delaying gratification in the pursuit of more meaningful goals and pursuits. We parents, for example, can seldom take shortcuts. We need to keep working hard, even on bad days, on the important challenges in life, such as school, work, raising children, and improving the world.

Here is a sample conversation that encourages Laura to be more persistent.

Father: How is basketball going?

Laura: I'm not as good as Maira at shooting. I think I'll try something else.

Father: It takes a lot of practice to get good. Sometimes years.

Laura: Years? I don't have years. I don't even have months. What's an easier sport?

Father: They all take practice and perseverance.

Laura: What's that?

Father: It means you stick to it over time. You keep trying. Most sports and, well, most important things that you do take time and practice.

Laura: I guess I could try basketball a little longer.

Father: Remember, even pro players miss about half the time. And they get paid a lot of money!

Laura: Will you pay me money to make baskets?

Father: No.

Good at Making Good Decisions

Making good decisions is a vital trait for life because there are so many important decisions to make. Your child must learn how to weigh and compare all the possible choices or sides. In many cases, you child will have to make a decision whether or not to buy something, do a certain job, help someone in need, and so on. Life will be full of decisions, and he or she must be well practiced in making the best choices that he or she can make.

What makes a decision good, though? The term *good* will mean different things at different times to different people. But most of the time, it will meet one or more of the following criteria:

- It is best choice for the mental or physical health and happiness of others.
- It is the most socially responsible choice.
- It is the safest choice.
- It is the most practical choice.
- It is the least costly choice in terms of money, time, energy, resources.
- It is the "heaviest," most logical choice after weighing the quantity and quality of evidence and reasoning on each side.
- It is best choice for one's own mental or physical health and happiness.

Of course, over time it is important to have conversations that help students to develop abilities to use these types of criteria and not just focus on the same one all the time. A large part of being able to make good decisions is being fair, logical, and unbiased.

Here is a short conversation sample focused on helping Gavin make good decisions.

Father: So, Gavin, what do you think about where we should go on vacation? We can go to the mountains or the lake. Before you decide, let's talk about them both. Maybe we start with mountains. What are the good things?

Gavin: They're not as hot. I like to walk around and go up to the top.

Father: Yeah, mountains have many advantages. They are often cooler in the summer because they are high up and the air is cooler. They are very pretty and there's great hiking. But what about bad things up in the mountains?

Gavin: Mosquitoes. They're the worst. And they are a long drive.

Father: Yes, I don't like mosquitoes either. Or the drive. So now the lake. What are good things?

Gavin: It's closer, less driving. It is warm water to swim in. I like to go fishing, but the fish are small.

Father: And I also like the barbecues we have on the shore. The food tastes so good, and the picnics. But what about the negative things?

Gavin: Small fish. And it can get hot in the tent.

Father: Yeah. But I don't even care if I catch a fish because it is so peaceful. No cars, no stress. But the mosquitoes are no fun, and you might get bored just sitting around. So where should we go? What has more positives and fewer negatives?

Gavin: I think the lake.

Notice how Gavin's father got him to think about the positives and negatives of each choice to then make a decision based on what he considered to be the heaviest reasons. This is an example of developing in a child the vital life skill of building up both (all) sides of an argument before taking a side and simply trying to win. The more that we can model, through conversation, this more objective and rational way of making decisions and choosing sides of an argument, the more we prepare our children to become fair and logical members of society.

SUMMARY

This chapter focused on nurturing and sculpting your child's heart through conversation. It emphasized ways to foster positive and helpful feelings while reducing and controlling the negative ones. It also looked at how to use conversation to develop traits and values that will help your child in school and in life.

About the Author

Jeff Zwiers, Ed.D., is a senior researcher at the Stanford Graduate School of Education and the director of professional development for the Understanding Language initiative. He has taught in diverse elementary and secondary schools. His research consists of collaborating and co-teaching with teachers and parents to learn what works best for educating all learners. He has also written numerous books and articles on literacy, thinking, communication, conversation, and language development. He lives with his wife and two very conversational children in Northern California.

CPSIA information can be obtained
at www.ICGtesting.com
Printed in the USA
LVHW111646130921
697671LV00012B/5

9 781475 860542